Janet Marshall trained as a teacher at Matlock College of Higher Education, 1979–82. Having specialized in Religious Studies and English with Drama, she then taught RE in two London secondary schools. She worked briefly as a support teacher/instructor in Cambridge in psychiatric care and for Church Army in central London in hostels for the homeless, before returning to primary teaching in Derby in 1989. Janet taught at an inner-city junior school in Derby until she took up her current post of Education Officer at the Anglican Shrine, Walsingham, in 1996, where she was responsible for the setting up and development of the Education Centre. Today, Janet enjoys teaching the many schoolchildren who come through its doors and is a frequent visitor to schools, where she leads assemblies and shares her knowledge of Christian pilgrimage with children.

Published by
The Bible Reading Fellowship
First Floor, Elsfield Hall
15–17 Elsfield Way, Oxford OX2 8FG

ISBN 1 84101 372 2
First published 2005
10 9 8 7 6 5 4 3 2 1 0

Acknowledgments
Unless otherwise stated, scripture quotations are taken from the Contemporary English Version of the Bible published by HarperCollins Publishers, copyright © 1991, 1992, 1995 American Bible Society.

p. 89: Celtic Christian prayer is taken from the *Iona Abbey Worship Book 2001*, Wild Goose Publications, Glasgow

A catalogue record for this book is available from the British Library

Printed in Singapore by Craft Print International Ltd

Special people, special places

Making connections between Christian pilgrimage and everyday life

Janet Marshall

This book is dedicated to Win and Mabel Moore, RIP.
I thank them for bringing the Bible alive to me,
for leading me, loving me and nurturing me on my
pilgrimage of faith and life for so many years.

Acknowledgments

With thanks to:

All Education Officers, Visits Officers and their departments at the various cathedrals and shrines mentioned in this book, for all their help, support and information.

The Revd Philip North, Grace Brodie and the Education Department Management Committee at the Shrine of Our Lady of Walsingham, for their continued encouragement and support while writing this book, and in my work as a whole.

Sue Doggett at BRF, for her continuous support and patience.

Martin Palmer and Nigel Palmer, authors of the book *Sacred Britain*, which was an invaluable resource in the writing of this book.

Preface

Pilgrimage is a wide-reaching concept. In essence it is about *making journeys*.

It starts with us. We all share a common pilgrimage—life! Life is a journey. It is not a solitary journey; it is one that we all share with those around us. Life is never static; we are continually growing, changing and moving. For Christians, there is also the important belief that pilgrimage continues after earthly lives have ended, that the spiritual part of our being continues on another heavenly journey to everlasting life with God.

Cardinal Basil Hume OSB had this to say about pilgrimage:

Life is a pilgrimage... So here I am, a pilgrim through life, restless indeed, looking, searching all the time for that which will make me truly and fully myself... The way is often rough for a pilgrim and hard going, but pilgrims must keep going resolutely and courageously. They are lost if they stop looking for the right way to reach their destination.

FROM *TO BE A PILGRIM: A SPIRITUAL NOTEBOOK* (TRIANGLE, 1988)

Another contemporary Christian writer, Brother Ramon SSF, wrote, 'We all go on pilgrimage. It is part of our human yearning to associate places with people we love, with experiences which are precious, with events which are holy' (from *The Heart of Prayer*, Zondervan, 1995).

Pilgrimage is also about places—special, holy destinations that lie at a journey's end. These places have often become sacred for individual believers because they experienced a desire to serve God in a particular way while they were there.

Martin Robinson, in his book *Sacred Places, Pilgrim Paths: an Anthology of Pilgrimage* (Zondervan, 1998), writes:

Pilgrimage sites are associated with holy people, with saints, sometimes in the sense of the presence of relics, or with the miraculous, for example, the location of visions or healing events. Acts of healing are often sought and sometimes reported by pilgrims... The hopeful traveller seeks to meet with the holy as a means of bringing meaning to this life.

There is nothing new about pilgrimage. It has been a feature of religious belief all over the world for hundreds of years. It is not something that is exclusive to Christianity. It is a key part of many world faiths.

The first recorded Christian pilgrimage to Jerusalem was around AD170. The pilgrim was a man named Melito of Sardis. He wanted to see for himself the places written about in the Gospels. The great Christian writer Jerome said that he felt a visit to the Holy Land would enable pilgrims to understand scripture better. The emperor Constantine gave state recognition to pilgrimage by excavating sites in Jerusalem that were of particular interest to Christians. He then marked these sites by building magnificent churches.

Desert pilgrimages also became popular in those early years. Christian hermits and monastic communities began to make journeys into the desert in Egypt. It was thought that the Christian faith had become too worldly and there was therefore a need to 'retreat' into the desert to escape the world and pray for it. Many of these early pilgrims were monks and nuns.

Pilgrimage gradually spread. Missionary monks known as 'ascetics' on the outer fringes of Western Europe began to make pilgrimage more imaginative. The Celtic ascetics, who later became saints, saw pilgrimage as a spiritual adventure. They set sail in boats called coracles and allowed the wind of the Spirit to take them wherever it would. It was also about mission, spreading the gospel of Jesus Christ. Wherever their boat landed would be the place to start spreading the gospel message.

Other Celtic saints, such as Cuthbert of Lindisfarne, planned specific destinations for their journeys, in order to spread the gospel. For these pilgrims, pilgrimage was about leaving their homelands and setting out with a purpose into the unknown. They were making these journeys for Jesus, to take his message to places where it was yet unknown. They were also imitating what Jesus himself did during his ministry: he travelled from place to place, teaching and caring for others.

By medieval times, pilgrimages had become important acts of faith. People made pilgrimages to holy places in order to develop their own spiritual lives. Pilgrimage journeys were often long and arduous. Many were sent on them as a penance—punishment for their wrongdoings. It was a popular punishment for thieves and murderers. They had to obtain a certificate from the holy site to prove they had actually got there. Wealthy pilgrims often paid others to go on pilgrimages on their behalf, to offer prayers for them at holy sites.

So what is pilgrimage all about in the 21st century?

Does it still have a part to play in the lives of modern-day Christians? In short, the answer is yes! This book aims to bring alive ten pilgrimage sites in Great Britain that are still popular destinations for today's Christian pilgrims. Indeed, there are busy sites of pilgrimage all over the world.

What is the difference between a pilgrimage and a 'holy holiday'? After all, the word 'holiday' comes from 'holy day'. Throughout history, pilgrimages to holy sites have held even more significance when undertaken on holy days. For example, pilgrims to the Shrine of St James in Compostela, Spain, always used to aim to arrive on the feast of St James, 25 July. Many pilgrims today use a pilgrimage as a time to unwind and relax, to explore the area around the site.

But is a pilgrim just another type of tourist? The main difference between a pilgrim and a tourist is that a pilgrim seeks to be changed by the experience of pilgrimage. The journey is an important part of that experience. It is a time to reflect and prepare so that the pilgrim is then ready to offer himself or herself to God in prayer on arriving at the holy place. The time spent there will then be a time of reflection about his or her life. Many pilgrims see it as a time to recharge their spiritual batteries, ready to go back to their busy working or home lives again, strengthened and renewed. At particular sites there may be a special focus on healing and renewal.

Pilgrimage is a fascinating topic and it is very much 'alive and kicking' for Christians today. This book aims to bring it alive for children. It seeks to inform and inspire teachers of Key Stage 2 to enable them to introduce their children to this exciting and challenging concept as part of their RE lessons. It seeks to introduce places of pilgrimage across Britain that are still important for Christians today.

It is well worth taking the children on visits to cathedrals, shrines and other places of pilgrimage. There is nothing like experiencing the places and meeting the people for whom they are special today. There are ten sites featured in this book and most of them have education departments. Details about the services they offer to schools are set out in the relevant sections of the book.

Children are fascinated by pilgrimage, and I hope you enjoy exploring it with your children as much as I do.

Janet Marshall

Contents

Foreword

For many Key Stage 2 teachers, *Special People, Special Places* is set to become an invaluable and time-saving resource for teaching about Christianity as part of their Religious Education scheme of work. It contains fascinating background information presented in a variety of accessible ways for pupils.

The book sets out to unpack the concept of pilgrimage, be that to a shrine or the journey through life itself, and it does so very successfully. Some teachers will be fortunate enough to live in an area of the country that boasts one of the key shrines studied. For others, the book provides a model for investigating sacred places nearer to home. The content of the book is such that it also spills over into other areas of the RE curriculum and can be used flexibly in many KS2 topics: for example, worship, inspirational people, symbolism and religious expression, vocation and lifestyle, religion and the individual.

I am sure that you will enjoy sharing this book, with all its facts, stories and thoughts, with your pupils. They give much scope for reflection. Indeed, if we allow them to, they may say something to each of us on our own ongoing journey through life.

Helen Matter
RE Adviser for Norfolk; Suffolk Advisory Teacher for RE

How to use this book

This book is a resource for teachers of Key Stage Two to introduce and explore the wide-ranging concept of pilgrimage.

All the material is curriculum-linked in order to supplement teaching of various units of study in County syllabi and in the QCA units for RE. Specific links are set out below and throughout each section.

The book is set out in three sections that follow on from one another sequentially in order to extend the children's knowledge and understanding of the concept of pilgrimage. The three sections comprise:

- Section 1: Life as a journey
- Section 2: Christians on the move: pilgrimage sites across Britain
- Section 3: Pilgrimage in the Bible

SECTION 1: LIFE AS A JOURNEY

This section begins where the children are. Through stories and activities they are encouraged to look at their lives as a journey and explore ways in which relationships, places and experiences shape us as people who are constantly growing and developing spiritually as well as physically.

NB: It is advisable to work through the whole of Section 1 in the order that it appears so that the concept might be introduced thoroughly.

Curriculum links

Non-statutory national framework: RE KS2 Knowledge, skills and understanding

- Learning from religion e: Pupils should be taught to reflect on sources of inspiration in their own and others' lives.

Breadth of study

- Religions and beliefs a: Christianity.
- Themes e: Beliefs and questions: how people's beliefs about God, he world and others impact on their lives.
- Themes h: The journey of life and death: why some occasions are sacred to believers, and what people think about life after death.
- Experiences and opportunities p: Considering a range of human experiences and feelings.
- Experiences and opportunities q: Reflecting on their own and others' insights into life and its origin, purpose and meaning.
- Experiences and opportunities r: Expressing and communicating their own and others' insights through art and design, music, dance, drama and ICT.

SECTION 2: CHRISTIANS ON THE MOVE

This section is in two parts. Part 1 introduces the concept of special and holy places through stories and activities. It also introduces the fact that pilgrimage has taken place for hundreds of years. Through the eyes of Master Cedric, a medieval pilgrimage group leader, children are encouraged to think about what pilgrimage was like at that time. There are suggested follow-up activities. Part 2 offers introductory information and a range of texts and activities on ten pilgrimage sites across Britain.

NB: If time is limited, you may wish to select particular pilgrimage sites. You may, for example, wish to prioritize a site that is geographically closest to your area of the country, so that follow-up visits can take place. A selection of sites that are further afield could follow this study. Alternatively, you may wish to introduce the children to all ten of the sites outlined in this book. The sites may be explored in any order. Some sites may link with particular history topics you are teaching.

Curriculum links

Non-statutory national framework: RE KS2
Knowledge, skills and understanding

- Learning about religion d: Pupils should be taught to investigate the significance of religion in local and national communities.
- Learning about religion e: Pupils should be taught to consider the meaning of a range of forms of religious expression, understand why they are important in religion and note links between them (for example, pilgrimage and prayer).
- Learning from religion e: Pupils should be taught to reflect on sources of inspiration in their own and others' lives.

Breadth of study

- Religions and beliefs a: Christianity.
- Religions and beliefs c: A religious community with a significant local presence, where appropriate.
- Themes e: Beliefs and questions: how people's beliefs about God, the world and others impact on their lives.
- Themes g: Worship, pilgrimage and sacred places: where, how and why people worship, including at particular sites.
- Themes j: Inspirational people: figures from whom believers find inspiration.
- Themes k: Religion and the individual: what is expected of a person in following a religion or belief.
- Experiences and opportunities n: Encountering religion through visitors and visits to places of worship, and focusing on the impact and reality of religion on the local and global community.
- Experiences and opportunities p: Considering a range of human experiences and feelings.
- Experiences and opportunities r: Expressing and communicating their own and others' insights through art and design, music, drama and ICT.

QCA units 2000

- Unit 5D: How do the beliefs of Christians influence their actions?
- Unit 3E: What is faith and what difference does it make? (In particular section 3: the impact of faith/ responses to stories of faith.)
- Unit 4B, section 1: Christmas journeys: pilgrimage.
- Unit 6E: What can we learn from Christian religious buildings?

SECTION 3: PILGRIMAGE IN THE BIBLE

This section explores pilgrimage-like biblical journeys that had life-changing consequences for the characters involved. The aim is to show how the concept of pilgrimage stretches throughout the Bible story. The material explores the stories of:

- Noah's obedient response when God asked him to set off on a journey into the unknown.
- Moses, who was called by God to lead the Israelites through the desert on a journey of risk and bravery.
- Jesus' pilgrimage to Jerusalem as a child and how Mary and Joseph discovered what a special person he was growing up to be.
- Jesus' choice of his first disciples and how they each embarked on a personal pilgrimage. They left their homes behind to travel around with Jesus.
- How Paul was travelling to Damascus when God called him in a very dramatic way. He then embarked on many journeys to tell others about Jesus.

Curriculum links

Non-statutory framework: RE KS2
Breadth of study

- Religions and beliefs a: Christianity.
- Themes f: Teachings and authority: what sacred texts and other sources say about God, the world and human life.
- Themes j: Inspirational people: figures from whom believers find inspiration.
- Experiences and opportunities r: Expressing and communicating their own and others' insights through art, design, music, dance, drama and ICT.

QCA units 2000

- Unit 6C: Why are sacred texts important?
- Unit 3D: What is the Bible and why is it important for Christians?

ACTIVITIES

All three sections suggest various activities to help extend and consolidate each topic area. Many of these activities can be linked to English and drama units.

SECTION 1

Life as a journey

Part 1

The journey of life

This section aims to introduce the concept of life as a journey. A series of short stories are offered which introduce two characters, Granny Roberts and William, a nine-year-old boy.

The stories are intended for reading aloud to the whole class or to small groups. You could use them as discussion starters, and it is hoped that they will motivate children to look at their own 'life journey' so far and to appreciate the life journeys of others around them, especially older members of their families and local communities.

During discussions, children can also be encouraged to think about how Christians believe that God knows, loves and treasures each person, both before they are born and during their whole life journey. This is an important concept to explore in preparation for later sections of this book, which explore ways in which Christians believe God has powerfully affected and intervened in people's lives throughout history. The ways in which this has been fundamental in spreading the Christian faith as well as creating 'holy' places across Britain, many of which have become places of pilgrimage, will also be explored.

You may wish to use this section as a starting point for introducing Christian rites of passage such as baptisms and funerals. The Christian church offers these special ceremonies to mark and celebrate the point at which a child or adult becomes part of the Christian family and when they leave it at the end of their earthly life. It is also a means of reminding Christians how special and unique each individual is to God and to offer a way of celebrating and giving thanks for this.

Some children may have lived in the same home for the whole of their lives. Others may have moved house, town or village like the boy in the story. Some families may originate from another area, culture or country. The whole issue of moving and changing lifestyles can be discussed.

Key teaching points based on the stories and activities

- Each child/adult is unique and special.
- Each of us is on our own individual journey of life and we share our journeys with those around us in our families, schools, places of work and local communities.
- Growing, learning, changing and 'moving on' are all part of life's journey.
- People, relationships and places affect our journey and the journeys of others.

NB: It is advisable to remind children of the dangers of forming relationships with strangers or entering a stranger's house. William, the boy in the story, and his parents know Granny Roberts personally and William visits her with the agreement of his parents.

William finds a granny

William lived next door to Granny Roberts. She was one of his best friends. Granny Roberts was not his real grandmother. In fact, she had no children of her own. William did not have any grandparents of his own either, because they had all died before he was born.

When William and his parents came to live in Bluebell Drive, he was five years old. He could still remember the day the removal van parked outside their new house. Granny Roberts was cleaning her bay window. They were following behind the van in their car. As soon as the car stopped, William threw open the door and ran up the drive towards their new front door.

'Careful, Will!' shouted his mum.

'Hello. You must be my new neighbours,' called Granny Roberts. 'I've been looking forward to meeting you,' she said with a beaming smile.

William's parents introduced themselves.

'I'm Mrs Roberts,' she told them. 'And what's your name, then, young man?' she asked.

William told her his name and from that moment William knew they were going to be friends.

'Call me Granny Roberts,' she said.

'Ooh, can I, Mum?' asked William excitedly.

'Well, if you're sure, Mrs Roberts,' said Mum.

'Oh, I'd like that very much,' she replied.

Granny Roberts brought round some delicious home-made biscuits and lemonade while they were unpacking, and that was the start of their very special friendship.

Questions for discussion based on this story

- How did Granny Roberts show friendship and caring for William and his family?
- In what way did her actions and her friendliness towards them help them to feel 'at home' in their new house?
- How might William have been feeling about moving house, starting a new school and making new friends?
- How might we help someone who has recently moved house or started attending our school?
- In what ways is it important to feel part of the community we live in?
- In what ways is your home a special place? Why?

This second story aims to help children explore further the importance of special people and relationships in their lives.

It's my birthday, Granny Roberts

Today was William's ninth birthday. It was on a Saturday and as soon as he had opened his presents he went straight round to Granny Roberts' house. He knocked on the door.

'Granny Roberts, Granny Roberts, it's me,' he yelled through the letterbox.

'Just a minute,' she shouted and he soon heard the familiar sound of her feet dragging along the hall in her furry slippers.

'Hello, young man,' she said as she opened the door. 'Happy birthday!'

William stepped into the hallway. It smelled of lavender. Granny Roberts always had a pot of it on her hall table. She said it was the best there was and it had come all the way from Norfolk. Granny Roberts often told William the story of how she bought it but he did not mind, as she always made it sound interesting.

'Well, young man, how does it feel to be nine?' asked Granny, reaching up on top of her bookcase, where there was a rather interesting parcel.

'Well, I don't really feel any different,' said William.

'Oh my, I wish I was nine again!' said Granny with a chuckle.

Granny gave William his present. It was a shiny red fire engine with a ladder that pulled right out on top of it.

'Oh, thank you, Granny! It's just what I wanted,' he shrieked.

'Well, a little bird told me you might want one of those!' she said, laughing again.

They both sat down to eat some toast with Granny's yummy strawberry jam on it.

'I wish I was grown up already, Granny,' said William while he was munching.

'Oh, William, don't you go wishing your life away!' exclaimed Granny Roberts. 'Eee now, we're never satisfied with where we are and what we've got,' she said with a cheeky giggle.

'You know, life is like a journey, William, and we move so fast on the journey, I sometimes wonder where on earth time has gone to.'

'Are you very old, Granny?' asked William.

'Well, it seems a long time since I was nine, that's for sure, young man,' she said with another chuckle.

'I don't like being *only* nine,' said William. 'I can't wait to be a grown-up!'

Granny got up slowly and headed towards her old oak bureau. The lid creaked as she pulled it down. She took out a sheet of paper and a pencil and brought it back to the dining-room table.

'Now, William, I think it's time we drew our "journey of life" wheel. Let's see just how much you've got from your life's journey so far and where we're hoping to head from there. You know, life's very precious, young man, right here where you are now, and so are *you*. Have you ever thought—there's no one else in the whole world exactly the same as you! Now come on, let's start turning the wheel.'

Questions for discussion based on this story

- What would it be like to live without friends or people who care about us?
- Who are the people who are instrumental in helping us on our life journey?
- What responsibility does each of us have to help one another along the way?
- What things might older people have to offer children and young people, to help them as they grow up?
- What has happened on your journey of life so far?

Activity 1: Granny's journey of life wheel

You will need a copy of Worksheet 1 on page 80 for each child in class.

As suggested by Granny Roberts at the end of the story, children can be encouraged to look closely at their own journeys of life so far by creating a 'journey of life' wheel. Details of what they already know, or what they can find out, about the different stages of their life can be entered on the chart.

Alternatively, this activity could be presented as a whole class project. You will need a large sheet of white paper or thin card. Mark out the wheel shape and divide it into segments as shown on the activity sheet on page 80. Spread the paper or card sheet out on the playground or in the school hall so that each child can add to it. Other year groups could also be invited to contribute, as could school staff.

The children could also be encouraged to make 'journey of life' wheels at home with parents, carers, grandparents, aunts, uncles and other relatives or special people in their lives, to compare journeys. They could be encouraged to bring their completed wheels back into school and share what they have discovered about the life journeys of others.

Ask the children to question adults about how their life journeys have unfolded. Has life always progressed exactly as they planned it?

Activity 2: I'm a star!

This activity aims to help children look more closely at themselves as special and unique individuals. You will need a copy of Worksheet 2 (p. 81) for each child in the class.

Cut out the stars. Invite the children to fill in details about themselves, such as 'My name is...', 'My hair is...', 'My eyes are...', 'I am... years old', 'My hobbies are...', 'In my family there are... people'. Decorate the stars with pictures of significant events that have provided landmarks in their life. When the stars are completed, punch a hole at the top of each one and hang them up.

Activity 3: Journey of life display

Why not make a display and create a special area in the classroom? Display baby photographs, special belongings from when the children were younger, and photographs of events and so on, which form part of their journeys of life so far. Ask the question, 'What are the important landmarks so far on everyone's journey of life?'

Part 2

Special people, special places in our lives

This part aims to help introduce children to the importance of 'places' in our lives. Sometimes we are influenced in our lives by what happens in a particular place or by the nature of the place itself, as well as by the people who share the places with us. The children are invited to explore this concept through a story. It involves the characters Granny Roberts and her young friend William once again.

The aim of the story is to prepare children for thinking about sacred, holy places and people who have stories of faith associated with them. The following story may be read aloud as a discussion starter about special places in the children's own lives. Children may also wish to carry out a survey with older family members and teachers about their special places.

Key teaching points based on the stories and activities

- Encourage the children to question whether or not special places are important on our life's journey. Do the children themselves have special places they like to visit or have visited in the past, or special places where they like to spend time alone?
- Encourage discussion about what makes a place 'feel' special.
- Explore the importance of memories in our lives.
- Introduce the concept of a holy or sacred place.
- Begin to think about the sorts of holy places that are special for Christians and why.

Granny Roberts and the ice-cream cave

It was a very wet and windy Sunday afternoon and William was bored. He had played with his Lego, he had read his car magazines, he had learnt his spellings for Monday, and now he was *bored*.

'Can I go and see Granny Roberts?' he asked his mum.

'OK then, but don't make a nuisance of yourself. Come straight home again if she has company,' said his mum.

William skipped out of the back door and over the low wall. He squashed his nose against Granny Roberts' sitting-room window. She was sitting in her favourite chair, knitting. William tapped the glass lightly.

'Oh! Come on in, pickle!' she shouted. William did not know why she called him this, and he did not like to ask her. Sometimes Granny Roberts said some funny things. It was just her way.

William opened Granny's back door and ran through into the sitting-room.

'What's to do then, William?' she asked with a big beaming smile.

'I'm bored,' said William.

'Bored!' she exclaimed. 'Eee, I was never bored at your age and we never had all the toys and gadgets you have these days! I tell you what, let's get my old photo albums out, shall we?'

Granny stood up slowly. She complained a lot about her knees aching these days. She said it was the cold and draughts that got into her bones. She went over to her huge bookcase by the piano and pulled out a large, shabby, faded green book. On it was written 'Weston Super Mare 1932'.

'Now, this was my mother's album and I can just about remember this holiday,' she said with a smile. 'I was seven, William.'

Granny sat down again with a groan and opened the album. It had a fusty smell.

'Where have all the colours gone?' asked William, as he looked at the photos on the front page.

'Oh, we didn't have any colour photographs when I was young—and you should have seen the size of the old box camera! Umm, I think I still have it in the loft somewhere.' Granny turned the pages slowly.

'Now, here we are…' she said with a grin. 'The day we went to the ice-cream cave.'

'The ice-cream cave!' shouted William.

'Yes, that's it! Oh, I thought it was a magical place that summer and it became my most treasured place, that cave, until I was grown up, William.'

William noticed that there were tears in Granny's eyes when she said this, although she was still smiling. There on the page William saw a little girl in a frilly bathing costume, sitting on a rock by the side of a cave. He could see that there was also a beach, and the sea was in the distance. The little girl was holding an enormous ice-cream in her hands and she was laughing.

'Who's that?' asked William

'Why, that's me!' chuckled Granny Roberts. 'I've changed a bit since then, haven't I?'

Granny then began to explain about her special cave.

'We went to Weston Super Mare every summer. I used to stay with my mum and dad in a little guesthouse on the sea front. Well, one day it was so hot. I'd been playing on the beach and my mum was sitting there with a scarf over her head under her sun umbrella. I'd been making sandcastles, I'd eaten my lunch and I was bored, and very hot. "Betty, why don't you go down for a paddle in the cove over yonder?" my mum said to me. I think I was beginning to get on her nerves with my whinging! So off I went. My dad had gone off for a stroll about a half an hour before.

'When I got to the cove, the water there was as clear and sparkling as a diamond. I put my toe in the water and it was so cool. Then I saw the cave. It looked dark but I was a one for adventure in those days so I decided to step inside. It was so cool as I stepped in! Oh, it was lovely after being so hot and bothered. Then I saw them…'

Granny's voice stopped suddenly, making William jump.

'Saw what, Granny?' he asked hesitantly.

'The ice-creams!' she exclaimed. 'There they were in a row, three pots of them on a rock in the centre of the cave... strawberry, vanilla and chocolate.' Granny's eyes lit up as she said this, and William could see a little tear starting to form again.

'What happened next?' asked William eagerly.

'Well, I couldn't believe my eyes at first! I stepped towards them and I stuck my finger into the strawberry one. Oooh, it was delicious! Then I heard my dad's voice behind me. "Think you'll be needing this, madam," he said, holding out a little wooden scoop. "Welcome to the magic ice-cream cave," he said. So that's me in the photograph, you see, eating that wonderful ice cream!'

'Was it really a magic cave, Granny?' asked William.

'Well, I believed it for many a year, young man. And then, when I was about ten, my mum told me it was really Dad who had gone on ahead that day and put the ice-creams there for me to find! But to me it was always a special cave. It became my favourite thinking spot. I always looked forward to going there, especially when I needed to chew things over in my mind or make important decisions. Things always seemed to come right after I'd had a think in that cave. I often used to say a prayer in there to God as well, William. Yes, some places are just special,' said Granny Roberts with a smile as she closed the album.

Questions for discussion

- Was it just the 'place' that was special for Granny Roberts?
- In what ways do people help to make a place special or memorable?
- Places are often associated with emotions or treasured memories of people we know. Is this important? In what ways were Granny Roberts' memories important to her?
- What memories do the children have of people who are special to them that are associated with a particular place?

Ask the children about their own personal special places—perhaps their own rooms at home, or an outdoor location. Have they a holiday destination that they really enjoyed visiting? What is it that makes a place special?

Do we all need time, spaces and places to think in at times, or even to pray in? What sorts of special places do Christians use to think in, worship in and talk to God in?

Granny Roberts said she often said a prayer in the cave. Do you think it is important for Christians to have special 'holy' places to worship and pray in, or can worship and prayer take place anywhere? Are the people just as important, more important, or not so important as the place itself when worship is taking place?

NB: It might prove useful to make a note of comments, opinions and feelings expressed by children at this stage. The children may even find it useful to log their findings as a result of discussions that have taken place about holy places for Christians. It would be interesting to come back to these and see if their opinions or feelings have changed after they have explored pilgrimage to holy places in the forthcoming sections of this book, and perhaps once they have visited some holy places for themselves.

Activities

The children could follow up the discussion by painting or drawing their special place. They could write a poem about it and what makes it special.

Alternatively, the children could compile a book of all the special places shared by class members. Perhaps they could be invited to bring in photographs of special events, places, holidays or people. The children could be encouraged to share verbally with each other what these places mean to them personally and then write about them in the class book.

Children might also enjoy interviewing or video-recording older family members or local people who could come into school to talk about their special memories of places or things that have happened. The children could make a CD for the school library or IT resources.

They could write a story about an imaginary place that is very special for an individual person or group of people. By way of introduction to this, examples could be shared of special places such as Narnia in C.S. Lewis' stories, or Hobbiton in *The Lord of the Rings*, or the garden in the book *The Secret Garden*. Excerpts from videos showing the movie versions of these books could be shown to the class to give them ideas, or portions could be read from the stories.

Examples could also be offered of epic journeys people have made, such as Dame Ellen MacArthur's boat trips round the world or the journeys of other famous explorers or mountaineers like Joe Simpson. (Ask your local library for help in locating books about these or other people who have accomplished ambitious journeys.) Encourage the children to discuss with one another how these experiences affected those individuals. Why did they feel compelled to make such journeys? What did the experience mean to them?

Start to think about holy places in your own neighbourhood, holy places the children have visited, or places around the country which have significance as holy sites. Look at some pictures of different styles of churches, cathedrals and other religious buildings. Pictures of holy buildings associated with other world faiths could also be looked at, such as mosques, temples, gurdwaras and so on, to point out that it is not just Christians who have special holy places to worship in. Is what the building looks like on the outside and the inside important? Visit local places of worship to compare and contrast.

SECTION 2

Christians on the move: pilgrimage sites across Britain

Part 1

Introducing pilgrimage

The overall aim of this section is to introduce children to the concept of pilgrimage as a special journey to a destination believed to be 'holy'. It will also introduce the fact that people have been making pilgrimage journeys for hundreds of years in Britain. It is intended that the children will gain a basic understanding of pilgrimage in order to begin exploring the history and function of ten Christian sites of pilgrimage across Britain.

There are various suggested activities in this section, including a story, which again features the characters of Granny Roberts and William. This time, Granny Roberts recalls a memorable pilgrimage that she made to the Holy Land, which was extremely important for her as a Christian. Many Christians make pilgrimages to the Holy Land to follow in the footsteps of Jesus—the key figure of Christianity.

It is hoped that children will be encouraged to think about how important and special Jesus is for Christians in their lives. The story is intended to be read aloud to the class or to small groups.

Key teaching points based on the stories and activities

- Pilgrimage forms part of many world faiths.
- Christians all over the world make pilgrimages to special 'holy' places, but these are not necessarily churches or buildings.
- The word 'pilgrimage' means a journey to a special 'sacred' or 'holy' destination. Both aspects are important: the journey is for preparation and the destination is for the pilgrims to offer themselves and their prayers to God.
- Pilgrimage is nothing new! It has taken place for hundreds of years and still takes place today.

Granny Roberts goes on pilgrimage

It was Friday evening at last. William had been ticking the days off on his calendar for two whole weeks.

'Granny Roberts comes home tonight,' he said to his mum at tea-time. 'I can't wait to see her! It seems ages since she went away on this Bril-gim-ige,' he continued while he was munching his beans on toast.

'It's a PIL-GRIM-AGE, Will!' answered his mum, giggling as she said it.

'Well, I've missed her, Mum. It just isn't the same when she's away,' answered William indignantly.

'Yes, I know, Will. I do hope she's been OK while she's been away. Her knees were very sore before she left and I expect she has been doing lots of walking,' said his mum.

'She was so looking forward to it, Mum. She said it was a journey she had been wanting to make for years and years. She said she was going to visit all the places Jesus lived and worked in,' said William, gulping down his last mouthful.

'That's right, Will, she's been to Israel—or the Holy Land, as many people call it. That's where Jesus lived. Lots of people go on pilgrimage there.'

Suddenly there was the sound of a car horn outside. William jumped to his feet and ran to the window.

'She's back, Mum! Look, there's a taxi outside! She's ba-ack, she's ba-ack,' he sang as he ran full-speed along the hall and out of the front door.

Granny Roberts was easing herself slowly out of the car as William jumped on her and threw his arms round her neck.

'Hello, Granny Roberts, I'm so glad you're home!' he yelled.

'Oh, steady on now, anyone would think you'd missed me!' said Granny with a tired voice. 'Now come on, young man, make yourself useful and carry some of my bags into the house for this nice taxi driver.'

Granny was very tired that evening, so William's mum made her a cup of tea, then told William to leave her alone until the next day. 'She needs an early night, Will,' she said. 'It's been a very long journey.'

Next morning, straight after breakfast, William could hardly wait to get round to Granny's house. He wanted to find out all about this pilgrimage. Granny was sitting at her dining-room table when he arrived, with a pile of postcards and all sorts of interesting objects in front of her.

'Now sit down here, William, my lad,' she said. 'I'll tell you all about it!'

Granny had explained before she went away that she had been saving up for a very long time to go on this special journey called a pilgrimage. Ever since she first became a Christian when she was a young woman, she had wanted to visit the country where Jesus was born and grew up, and the place where he died and rose again. Last year she'd heard that there was a group going to the Holy Land from her church, so she checked how much money she had in her savings account at the bank, and decided she had enough to pay for her flight and hotel.

'It's not the same as a holiday, William,' she'd explained before she set off. 'It's very special. I'll be following in Jesus' footsteps. I will be remembering all that he did in his life. I'll be reading stories about Jesus from the Bible in the places where they actually happened. I'll also be saying lots of prayers,' she'd said.

Now she was back!

'Have you had a good pil-gim-ige, Granny Roberts?' asked William excitedly.

'*Pilgrimage*, William, the word is *pilgrimage*. Oh yes, I've had a wonderful time. We said some prayers before we set off, to get our minds ready for all the places we were going to be visiting. We asked God to keep us safe on the journey, too. It was a very long journey, William. Israel is hundreds of miles away.'

'Wow!' said William.

'Oh, William, I can't explain how wonderful it all was. I visited Bethlehem, where Jesus was born. Then we went to Nazareth, where Mary was visited by the angel Gabriel and found out she was going to give birth to God's son Jesus,' explained Granny.

'We did that in our nativity play at school last Christmas, Granny!' exclaimed William.

'I know you did. You were a shepherd, William. Do you know, I even visited the shepherds' fields where they saw all the angels and the star in the sky!'

'Wow! That's cool, Granny!' said William.

'But the best bit for me, William, was walking through Jerusalem. We followed the way of the cross, William, the road Jesus walked along, carrying that heavy wood on his back to the hill where he was crucified. Look, here's a little wooden cross I was given, and I carried it all the way to help me think about Jesus.'

Granny Roberts picked up a little cross made of olive wood and placed it in William's hands.

'Keep this, William, it is very special. The priest blessed it in Jerusalem.'

'Wow! Thank you, Granny Roberts,' said William.

'How I walked all that way, I'll never know, with my knees!' said Granny. 'I just had to do it,' she added.

'What else did you see, Granny?' asked William.

'Oh, there was so much, William. You'll have to wait until I get my photos developed. Wait until you see me in the boat on the Sea of Galilee! It was a boat just like the one Jesus and his disciples sailed in, the day there was that bad storm at sea and Jesus told the wind and waves to be still. Do you remember that story, William?'

'Yes, I do, Granny,' he replied. 'You gave me that story for Christmas.'

'Well, I am so glad I have been able to go on this pilgrimage, William. I really feel I have visited some special *holy* places. You know I am a Christian, don't you, William?' she asked.

'Yes, Granny,' said William.

'Well, I feel a lot closer to Jesus now I've been to the places where he lived and worked and died. It's been very special, William,' said Granny with tears in her eyes.

'You look ever so tired, Granny,' said William.

'I am that—but here you are, now, I've brought you some sweets from Jerusalem and here's some olive oil from Nazareth for your mum.'

'Oh, thank you, Granny Roberts,' said William. He jumped up and gave her a kiss on the cheek. 'But this is my best present... having you home again!' he said as he picked up the bag of sweets.

'Yes, and I'm sure glad to see you again, William. Now run along. I think I need a little nap. See you again tomorrow!'

'See you, Granny,' shouted William as he headed towards the door.

'Pilgrimage, pilgrimage... I said it, I said it,' he chanted as he ran up the drive. 'I hope I can go on a pilgrimage one day!'

Questions for discussion based on this story

- Why was it so important for Granny Roberts to make this pilgrimage?
- Is a pilgrimage different from other journeys or holidays she might make? Why?
- Was this pilgrimage an important part of Granny's life journey?

NB: It is important that children start to gain awareness at this stage that pilgrimages form an important part of people's life journeys.

- Does Granny Roberts feel that her faith and her relationship with Jesus have been strengthened as a result of this pilgrimage?
- What do we mean by 'faith'?

Perhaps there are people within school, or from the local community, who could talk about a pilgrimage they have been on, or something else they have done that has affected their lives or their faith.

God's Son

Children can be encouraged to think about what Christians believe is so special about Jesus. Christians believe that Jesus was, and still is, God's Son. The word 'incarnation' can be introduced for older children.

- Ask the children if they can think of other special holy places in local communities where Christians can remember Jesus without going on a pilgrimage—for example, a church building.
- Could someone make a pilgrimage journey within a church building?
- What is a church for? (A place where Christians can gather together to remember Jesus, to pray to him and worship him.)

Activity 1: Postcards

Encourage the children to design or write a postcard from Granny Roberts to William, describing one of the holy places she has visited. The children could look at Holy Land brochures or pictures of various sites in that part of the world, to get an idea of the terrain and so on, and draw a scene on the postcard.

Activity 2: Advertising leaflets

The children could design a leaflet to advertise a pilgrimage to the Holy Land. Teachers may wish to write off to various pilgrimage tour companies for examples of promotional literature. Encourage the children to write about ways in which making the pilgrimage would help Christians in their lives and their faith.

Activity 3: Sacred space

Create a special place in the classroom with reminders about Jesus that are special to Christians—for example, crosses, crucifixes, statues, paintings, Bibles, rosary beads, prayer books and so on. Use this activity to emphasize to the children that having visual aids or pictures to remind Christians of their special friend, Jesus, and making pilgrimages to places that remind them of him, is similar to keeping photographs or mementos of special friends, relatives or pets, or visiting them because they are special to us in our everyday lives.

Pilgrimage in medieval times

This part offers a group reading which may be used as a whole-class or small-group activity, followed by discussion questions and a suggested written task. There is also a picture on Worksheet 3 (p. 82) for the children to colour, discuss and make notes on. This activity would be most effective if used in conjunction with Cedric's letter opposite. The picture aims to introduce children to pilgrimage in Britain in medieval times and to encourage them to think about how important it was in the everyday lives of Christians.

Key teaching points based on the stories and activities

- Most people in England were Christians in medieval times and their faith was very important to them.
- Everyone wanted to go on a pilgrimage. For those who were poor, it was a huge adventure and a chance to see other places and meet new friends.
- People believed that their prayers would be answered if they prayed at a shrine and they often took gifts or money to offer at the shrine.
- A 'shrine' is a special 'holy' place where people, including Christians, believe that God has made something special happen, or where they remember someone who has done very special things for God in his or her life.
- Shrines have become places of prayer and worship for people of many faiths, including Christianity.
- Christians hoped that when they died they would get to heaven more quickly if they had been on many pilgrimages to holy shrines during their lives. (Although unbiblical, this was a commonly held belief at the time.)

It may be useful to read the children a portion of *The Canterbury Tales* as an introduction to this section. There are various children's editions of this famous book about medieval pilgrimage to Canterbury. This will illustrate the different social classes of people who went on these journeys and what they got up to on the way. Ask the Education Department at Canterbury Cathedral for advice on children's versions and related resources (see p. 30 for contact details).

Look out for resources about pilgrimage. Your local RE resource centre may have books that you could borrow. It would be useful to show pictures of medieval pilgrims.

Investigate shrines in other world faiths, such as Hinduism.

Discussion questions and story to write

Think about the different sorts of pilgrims who might travel with Master Cedric and pretend you are one of them. Write a story about your journey. What kind of adventures do you have along the way?

Can you think of a modern-day person for whom you might choose to make a shrine—for example, someone who has done something special, a sportsperson, film or TV star, or just someone you know?

What sorts of things would you put in this shrine to help people to remember them? You might include photographs, or objects that remind people of that person.

Where would your shrine be and what would it look like?

Group reading activity: Meet Master Cedric, the pilgrim leader

Hello!

I am Master Cedric. I am a pilgrimage leader. I lived in England over five hundred years ago, back in medieval times. Look at my clothes. I am wearing the uniform of a pilgrimage leader.

Why do you think I wear a woollen cloak and a wide-brimmed hat? Why am I carrying a wooden staff?

It is my job to lead groups of pilgrims. Do you know how we travel to all the shrines around the country?

We walk! Sometimes a pilgrimage can last for many months. Often I find myself in charge of a very large group of pilgrims. People keep joining the group whenever we stop in a town or village. It is hard work sometimes. I have to make sure I know the way, and I have to make sure there are inns along the way so that we can stop off for food and a bed to sleep in at night.

Sometimes our journeys are very difficult, especially if we have to cross water or climb hills. Pilgrims usually make a will before they leave home, just in case they get sick and die on the journey.

All sorts of people join my pilgrimages. Sometimes there are noble knights, lords and ladies who are very rich. They travel on horses.

Town merchants travel with me, too. They often ride on donkeys. Many poor peasants also come along. I even have monks and nuns who join my group. I like my job because I get to meet so many interesting people.

I have to look out for pickpockets and criminals. Sometimes they sneak into the group, looking for rich nobles to steal from. Often they have been sent on pilgrimage as a penance. This means that they did something very wrong back home, such as stealing, so their priest sent them on a long pilgrimage as a punishment. When they reach the holy shrine they must get a certificate to prove that they got there. They must also say sorry to God there for their wrongdoings. Then they have to walk all the way home again.

It can be dangerous because often there are wild animals in our way, rivers to cross and mountains to climb. Sometimes we have to walk in wind, rain and snow. It is my job to make sure everyone stays safe and well on the journey. Sometimes people get very tired and miserable, so my minstrel, Hubert, plays them tunes on his pipes, and sings to them. He is a jolly fellow!

I always carry my Bible with me. Sometimes pilgrims do not know about Jesus, so I tell them stories from the Bible in the evenings. When we get to the shrine, it is my job to say a 'thank you' prayer to God for getting us there safely. People bring many prayers that they want to say in these special holy places, too.

I love visiting the beautiful churches and abbeys where many of the shrines are found. They are full of lovely things like crucifixes, statues, candles and paintings. Many of our rich noble pilgrims bring beautiful gifts to offer at the shrines. We all hope that our prayers will be answered quicker if we do this.

It's a great job being a pilgrim leader!

Part 3

Places of pilgrimage around Britain

This part features ten famous Christian pilgrimage sites across Britain. Teachers may choose as many or as few of these sites to look at with their children as they wish. The sites do not need to be covered in any particular order.

For each site, there is a teacher fact file, outlining historical background information and the story of why the site became a famous place of pilgrimage. This is followed by various activities, which aim to help bring the sites and their history alive for the children. Activities include dramatic readings, play scripts, poems, reading texts, activity sheets, questions for discussion, drama, art and craft ideas, dance and music.

You may wish to organize an educational visit to sites that are geographically accessible, or obtain further resources. Many sites have Education Departments attached to them and contact information is given for each site.

Key teaching points

- Christians do not have to travel to other countries to make pilgrimages. There are sites all over Britain that have been places of pilgrimage for hundreds of years. There are many sites across the country that have been given significance as holy places—places where people believe God has made his mark through a particular event or person.
- Such places became known as 'shrines'. It is important that children become familiar with this word.
- Christians still make pilgrimages to many of these sites.

Iona
Durham
Holywell
Chester
Lincoln
Walsingham
Bury St Edmunds
Westminster
Canterbury

Canterbury Cathedral, Kent: the Shrine of St Thomas à Becket

Teacher fact file

- Canterbury Cathedral is one of the greatest medieval buildings in the world.
- Canterbury Cathedral is the place where St Augustine brought Christianity back to south-eastern England in AD597.
- St Thomas à Becket became Archbishop of Canterbury in 1162, during the reign of Henry II.
- St Thomas was murdered and buried in the cathedral in AD1170. His tomb became the greatest shrine in Europe after St Peter's in Rome.
- Christians who prayed at his tomb claimed that miracle cures took place and prayers were answered.
- St Augustine was also buried in Canterbury Cathedral.
- Canterbury Cathedral is the spiritual 'Mother Church' of the Anglican Church across the world. Every ten years, the Lambeth Conference of bishops from across the world meets in Canterbury.
- The Archbishop of Canterbury (head of the Anglican Church in England) has his seat at the cathedral.
- Christians still make pilgrimages to Canterbury Cathedral. Staff there sometimes organize candlelit evening walks through the building, when the story of the martyrdom of St Thomas is told.

For resources and information about school visits to Canterbury Cathedral, contact the Education Department at Canterbury Cathedral. E-mail: schools@canterbury-cathedral.org

Activity 1: Under the sword!

The following drama activity aims to introduce children to the story of the martyrdom of St Thomas à Becket in 1170 and shows why Canterbury Cathedral subsequently became such an important and famous place of pilgrimage for Christians.

CAST

- ★ Narrator
- ★ Thomas of Canterbury
- ★ King Henry II
- ★ Knight 1 (Richard Brito)
- ★ Knight 2 (Hugh de Moreville)
- ★ Knight 3 (Reginald FitzUrse)
- ★ Knight 4 (William de Tracy)
- ★ Altar server
- ★ Priest

Narrator: This is the story of an unforgettable day. As dawn broke over Canterbury Cathedral, nobody there knew what terrible things were going to happen that day. Here's Archbishop Thomas. Let him begin the story…

Thomas: I was born in the year 1118. I had a happy childhood. My father was a rich London merchant. I came from a Christian family. We always went to church and I read the Bible. I enjoyed this so much that I decided to go to college in Paris when I was a young man to study the Bible. I was a clever student and when I had finished my studies I decided to become a knight.

In the year 1162, I became Archbishop of Canterbury. I said my prayers every day, but one day I got cross with King Henry and with other members of his court. Everyone seemed to be more interested in making money and having a good time than in following Jesus and saying their prayers. I told the king how I felt but he would not listen.

King Henry: Thomas, why are you upsetting everyone? You are my chief bishop. You must stop causing trouble! We want to enjoy life in my court. I am warning you, if you do not stop causing trouble, I will put you in prison.

Narrator: Thomas was scared. He ran away to France. After a while, the king asked him to come back.

Thomas: I am now back in Canterbury and I am Archbishop once again. Things are still not right in this country. I do not like the way our king is ruling the land. People are not following Jesus as they should in their lives. I keep telling the king but he will not listen.

Narrator: King Henry was getting very angry with Thomas and he started to think about how he could get rid of him. Four of his knights overheard him voicing his desire to be rid of Thomas.

King Henry: I am getting tired of Archbishop Thomas telling us what to do all the time. He will not keep quiet and I fear that I must do something about this soon.

Narrator: The knights knew that the king was very upset. They talked about how they could help him out.

Knight 1: We have to do something to make Thomas stop upsetting the king.

Knight 2: Why don't we arrest him and put him in prison?

Knight 3: If we do that, he will still speak out against the king.

Knight 4: If we kill him, that will put a stop to it all!

Knights 1, 2 and 3: Yes, we could do this for the king.

Narrator: The knights did not tell the king about their plans. Late that night, they set off on their horses from London to Canterbury. They arrived at the cathedral very early in the morning. As they peeped through the front doors, they saw the altar server and a priest getting ready for Mass at the altar. They crept quietly inside.

Knight 1: It looks as if Archbishop Thomas will be celebrating Mass this morning. He should be on his way in very soon.

Knight 2: Let's hide behind those pillars and wait until he gets to the altar.

Knight 3: Yes, have your swords ready. When he turns his back to us we can attack.

Narrator: The knights hid behind the huge stone pillars in the cathedral. Soon the bell rang for Mass and they saw Thomas walking in. As he walked up the altar steps, they jumped out and ran towards him with their swords shimmering in the early morning sunlight.

Altar server: No! No! Sirs, what are you doing?

Priest: Please, I beg you, put away your swords!

Narrator: It was too late. The knights pushed these men out of the way and ran towards Thomas with their swords. Thomas turned around.

Thomas: Dear Lord, please help me!

Narrator: But it was too late. Down came their swords and in a second he was dead. When news reached the king in London, he was shocked at what had happened.

King Henry: Why did they do this? I did not want this to happen.

Narrator: Everyone in the country was angry. Thomas was made a saint two years after his death and was buried in Canterbury Cathedral. A large stone tomb was built. Four years after his death, the king walked barefoot all the way to Canterbury to show how sorry he was for what had happened to Thomas. When he got to the tomb, he prayed there.

Priest: But that was not the end! People kept coming to visit St Thomas' tomb. It became a very famous holy shrine. Lots of people said that their prayers had been answered when they prayed there. Many said they had been cured of terrible illnesses. No one could ever have imagined that Thomas' murder would have led to this!

Narrator: Christian pilgrims still walk to Canterbury Cathedral to think about what happened to St Thomas and to see where he was murdered. Many walk there along a special country path called the Pilgrims' Way. Many still stand and say a quiet prayer to thank God for St Thomas' life. Some also pray to Thomas and ask him to help them in their lives, as they believe that he is in heaven and will hear their prayers and pass them on to God for them.

Activity 2: Class or small group discussion

- Why did Thomas not agree with the king?
- Why have Christians continued to have faith in St Thomas?
- Look again at what the people believed about answers to prayer they received when they prayed at his tomb.

Activity 3: Report writing

Children could write and present TV reports or Internet news reports to show the reactions of various groups of people to Thomas' murder.

Activity 4: Creative writing

Children could imagine that they are pilgrims visiting St Thomas' shrine or tomb, years after the event of his death. Poems and stories could be produced telling of miracles and answers to prayer that have taken place.

Activity 5: Design a stained-glass window

Children could design a stained-glass window for Canterbury Cathedral, to remind people of what happened to St Thomas.

Durham Cathedral: the Shrine of St Cuthbert

Teacher fact file

- Durham Cathedral houses the tomb of St Cuthbert. His body was brought here from his monastery in Lindisfarne in the year 995, after the monks had fled Lindisfarne under threat from Viking raids.
- At first, the cathedral was a small church called the White Church, built by the monks to house the tomb. It was then enlarged and a monastery was built too.
- Durham Cathedral became an important place of pilgrimage because of Cuthbert's tomb. It became a shrine.
- The Venerable Bede is also buried in the cathedral, in the Galilee Chapel. Bede was a monk from Jarrow who died in 735. He wrote the first history of England and many other books about saints. Bede wrote the life story of St Cuthbert.
- On the great north door there is a large Norman door knocker. It is in the shape of a lion's head and is known as the Sanctuary Knocker. This is a sacred sign that reminds people that this is a special, holy place.
- From 1464 until 1524, 331 people were given sanctuary in the cathedral. This means that the church gave them protection from the law. If they could reach up and grasp the knocker, they were entitled to 40 days' protection inside the cathedral. This ancient English right of sanctuary was abolished in 1623.

For resources and information about school visits to Durham Cathedral, contact the Education Officer.
E-mail: Elizabeth.baker@durhamcathedral.co.uk.
The official website for the cathedral is www.durhamcathedral.co.uk. Find out more about the Venerable Bede by visiting www.bedesworld.co.uk.
The education centre for Bede's World is www.bedesworld.co.uk/education-visits.php.

Activity 1: Sanctuary

There is an obvious link between the monks wishing to find sanctuary for the body of St Cuthbert and the door knocker, which offered a place of safety in the cathedral for people in danger or in trouble with the law.

This provides a useful and interesting opportunity to explore the whole concept of sanctuary with children, including issues presently affecting Britain and many other countries such as asylum seekers, human rights issues, racism, suffering and poverty around the world. This could be linked into work on Citizenship and RE units.

For resources and information about other agencies to contact for additional information, visit the following websites: www.christian-aid.org.uk; www.amnesty.org; www.redcross.org.uk; www.salvationarmy.org.uk.

Activity 2: Cuthbert's journey

This dramatic reading uses choral speaking to tell the story of how St Cuthbert came to Durham. Legend has it that Cuthbert's body was carried from Lindisfarne by the monks who were fleeing from Viking invasion. After wandering around the north of England and southern Scotland for seven years, they eventually laid his body to rest at Chester-le-Street near Durham. Here it remained for over a hundred years.

When new invasions were threatened, they again removed his body—this time to Ripon—but a few months later they carried it back to Chester-le-Street. On the way back, however, when the monks reached the place where the city of Durham now stands, their wagon came to a halt and would not move. Tradition has it that St Cuthbert appeared to them in a vision and indicated that he wished to be finally laid to rest on that very spot. This is why they buried him there and built the church.

After reading this piece together, you may wish to discuss the following points with the children:

- Why was it so important for the monks to put St Cuthbert's body in a safe tomb?
- Is it still important for people today to have a funeral and a special place to remember someone they love after that person has died? (Memories of a person always live on. Christians give thanks to God for someone's life when they die and they believe that the person's soul rests in peace with God.)

You may also wish to find out more about St Cuthbert's life and why he became such a famous saint.

CAST

- ★ Chorus (whole class or as many as you wish)
- ★ Voice 1
- ★ Voice 2
- ★ Voice 3
- ★ Voice 4

Chorus: *(Start quietly, then increase volume)*
Whoooosh... roar! Whoooosh... roar!
The waves were whirling all around.
Whooosh... roar! Whooosh... roar!
The waves were roaring all around.

Continue making a 'whoosh, whoosh' sound, rhythmically and quietly in the background, while Voice 1 is speaking the next line.

Voice 1: The boat set out one stormy day
with a special cargo stored away.
The little boat was tossed and blown
as the monks headed far away from home.

Chorus: *(Start quietly, then increase volume)*
Whoooosh... roar! Whoooosh... roar!
The waves were whirling all around.
Whooosh... roar! Whooosh... roar!
The waves were roaring all around.

Voice 2: Soon they reached the safe, dry land
where a wagon waited on the sand.
Cuthbert's body was placed inside
and they all set off on a long, long ride.

Chorus: And the wheels went round on the rocky ground.
And the wheels went round on the rocky ground.

Voice 3: Away from the Vikings they must go.
Quickly, horses, don't be slow!
They travelled around from town to town,
but they could not find safe resting ground.

Chorus: And the wheels went round on the rocky ground.
And the wheels went round on the rocky ground.

Voice 4: They wanted Cuthbert to rest safely soon,
but where could they build his final tomb?
Then they came to Durham town
and stopped to rest on the stony ground.

Chorus: They stopped to rest in Durham town;
the wagon stood still on the stony ground.
They stopped to rest in Durham town;
the wagon stood still on the stony ground.

Voice 1: One monk said, 'Brothers, it's time to go!
So come along now, don't be slow!
Let's get going while the sun still shines—
the resting place we're sure to find!'

Chorus: Heave ho, heave ho!
Heave ho, heave ho!

Voice 2: They pushed and pulled, but the wheels were stuck!
Stuck in a great big, dirty rut!
The wagon stood still on the dusty ground;
they were stuck in Durham town!

Chorus: Dig, dig, dig, dig! Dig, dig, dig, dig!
Dig, dig, dig, dig! Dig, dig, dig, dig!

Voice 2: They dug a grave and built a tomb;
they built a church, then very soon
a monastery and cathedral grand
they did build upon this land.

Chorus: So come on, pilgrims, head that way,
to Durham, hurry, don't delay!
Remember all who brought him there,
and stop to say a little prayer.

Activity 3: Do we need safe places (sanctuaries)?

This activity offers the opportunity for children to explore why symbols are important for giving information, reminding people of things, or encouraging them to think or pray. You could also use the activity to encourage children to think of a symbol of their own that they could use to communicate something important to them, such as being kind to one another, being a true friend and so on. Have a discussion about this to help them decide on the symbol they would use.

Follow up with a discussion about why the cross or crucifix is used by Christians as a symbol, and the significance of the other symbols on Worksheet 4 (p. 83).

Activity 4: Modern-day examples of sanctuary

Use the following information as a springboard for further discussion or research.

- Asylum seekers have taken refuge in churches in this country.
- Animals who are injured or species in danger of extinction are often placed in animal 'sanctuaries'.
- Should holy places like churches be places of sanctuary for people in need, even if they have broken the law?
- When modern-day pilgrims reach the north door at Durham Cathedral and see the Sanctuary Knocker, this gives them the opportunity to think and pray about all those people and creatures across the world who are in danger or need help—for example, in countries where there is war, violence or famine. What other symbols or objects could be placed in a church or other building, such as your school, to help people to think or pray?

Walsingham, Norfolk: the Shrine of Our Lady of Walsingham

Teacher fact file

- Legend tells us that the village of Walsingham in Norfolk has been a place of pilgrimage since medieval times.
- The legend of Walsingham, initially written as a ballad, tells of three visions of the Virgin Mary, mother of Jesus, and her house in Nazareth where the annunciation took place and where Jesus grew up. These visions were experienced by the then Lady of the Manor, Richeldis de Faverches, whilst she was praying.
- As a result of these visions, the legend goes on to say that a house was built miraculously during the night.
- A fresh water spring is also said to have appeared near the house, and Richeldis had it made into a well.
- The house became known as the Holy House or 'England's Nazareth' and soon became a place of pilgrimage and prayer. In the house was placed a statue of Mary, Our Lady of Walsingham, pointing to the Christ-child on her knee.
- Pilgrims also received water from the wells nearby and prayed for healing. Stories of miraculous cures quickly spread across the country.
- A community of monks, who were also known as Augustinian canons because they were ordained priests, came to Walsingham in 1153 to care for the house. They built a church over it, and a large priory church and monastery next door to it.
- The Holy House remained a busy pilgrimage site for Christians until the priory was dissolved in 1538 by King Henry VIII.
- A new Holy House with a pilgrim church around it was built a short distance away from the priory grounds in 1931. This was the idea of the parish priest at the time, Father Alfred Hope Patten.
- Thousands of pilgrims a year still visit the Holy House to pray. They still pray for healing and receive water from a Saxon well that was discovered on the site when the house was being built.
- There is also a Roman Catholic shrine in the nearby village of Houghton St Giles, the site of the medieval Slipper Chapel, where pilgrims used to stop to rest and give thanks before removing their shoes to walk the last holy mile to the Holy House. Many pilgrims still do this.

For resources and information about school visits to Walsingham, contact the Education Department on the Anglican shrine's website at www.walsinghamanglican.org.uk, email direct on ed@olw-shrine.org.uk or telephone 01328 824205.

A schools information pack is available from the Roman Catholic National Shrine (site of the famous ancient Slipper Chapel where medieval pilgrims prayed and removed their shoes before walking the final holy mile to the shrine). Telephone 01328 820217, or view the shared website www.walsingham.org.uk to gain further information about the Roman Catholic national shrine.

THE ANGLICAN SHRINE OF OUR LADY OF WALSINGHAM

Focus

Unlike many sites of Christian pilgrimage in medieval times, there were no tombs, martyrdoms or relics of saints (relics are objects associated with the saint) to be found in Walsingham. This time, the focus is on special events that took place there. Mary the mother of Jesus, a key figure in the Christian faith, chooses to visit (three times, in a vision) a local villager, Lady Richeldis de Faverches, in a particular place. Through these events, Richeldis is reminded that Jesus, God's Son, was born into this world through Mary and grew up in a family home with her and Joseph. The house becomes a symbol or reminder of this important Christian belief.

Christians call the event of Jesus' birth the incarnation—the time when God became a human being. All of this would have been in the minds of those early pilgrims, and this is still the focus of modern-day pilgrimage to the rebuilt Holy House within the Anglican Shrine church.

Activity 1: The Walsingham legend

In preparation for this activity about the Walsingham legend, you may wish to obtain a picture of the image of Our Lady of Walsingham and a painting, print or icon of the annunciation. Contact the Education Department at the Anglican shrine for information and assistance. Worksheet 5 (p. 84) is provided to enable the children to create an unfolding storyboard of the legend. You may wish to increase the size of the worksheet to A3 for each child.

This story could be adapted as a piece of drama to present in assembly or as a class project.

Hello. My name is Richeldis de Faverches. I am the lady of the manor. I am a Christian. I say my prayers every day. Life has not been easy for me lately. My husband died and I have a young son to bring up. His name is Geoffrey.

Picture 1

Pause for the children to colour in the picture of Richeldis de Faverches and her son, Geoffrey.

I must tell you about something that happened to me not long ago. It really changed my life! One day, I was in my room saying my prayers when, all of a sudden, I saw Mary the mother of Jesus in front of me. I rubbed my eyes... no, I was not imagining it! There she was! She was pointing to a house. I knew at once that this was Mary's house in Nazareth, where the angel Gabriel appeared to her and told her that she was going to be the mother of God's Son, Jesus, and where Jesus grew up.

Picture 2

Pause for the children to draw a picture of Richeldis de Faverches' vision of Mary, or an annunciation scene of the angel Gabriel visiting Mary in her house in Nazareth.

The next day, and the day after that, the same thing happened to me again. I had the same visions. I decided that Mary must want me to build a house, just like the one in Nazareth, right here in Walsingham. I had plenty of land near my manor house so I drew a picture of the house and called in our local carpenters straight away.

They came round to see me and I told them to get the best wood they could find. I showed them the drawing and told them to start building my house immediately.

They gave me a few funny looks, but off they went and they started to build.

Picture 3

Pause for the children to draw a picture of the carpenters building the house.

Late that day, my servant came to tell me that the carpenters needed to speak with me. 'They are having problems, my lady,' she said.

In they came. 'What's wrong?' I asked them.

'Well, it just will not go right, my lady,' they said. 'As fast as we put the wood together, it keeps falling down!'

I felt very cross and I told them to go home to bed. 'Come back early in the morning and get it finished!' I ordered them.

That night I could not sleep. I knelt by my bed and prayed all night long. I asked Mary in heaven to help me and I told God all about the problem. Just as dawn was breaking, I heard banging on my front door. 'Who can that be?' I thought. I opened the door myself and in ran the carpenters. They were so excited!

'My lady, it's been built. It's all done!' they shouted.

They explained that when they got to the field, there was the house, all perfectly built. I believed straight away that it was a miracle! God's angels had done this. I just knew it!

Picture 4

Pause for the children to draw a picture of the finished house and the surprised carpenters.

'This is a holy house,' I said. 'I want this to be a special place where people can come and pray whenever they want to. I am sure Mary will listen to their prayers here and she will pass them on to Jesus. I am going to put a statue of Mary with Jesus in here, to remind people of how special they both are.'

But that was not the end of the story. Oh no! Suddenly water gushed up from below the earth right next to my feet. A fresh water spring had appeared.

'This is another sign,' I told the carpenters. I told them to make it into a well straight away. 'I think people will be blessed by God when they drink water from this well,' I said.

Picture 5

Pause for the children to draw a picture of the water spring or the well.

Lots of people started to come to pray in my Holy House. People with terrible illnesses came to drink from the well. Lots of people said they had been cured. I knew that this was what Mary wanted. Every day now, people can come here and remember Jesus and his mother Mary. It has made me very happy.

Picture 6

Pause for the children to draw a picture of their own choosing.

Activity 2: Discussion starters

Christians still visit the present Holy House to offer prayers about their own lives and to say prayers for others. They light candles as a sign of their prayers. Medieval pilgrims did this too in the first Holy House. They do it because they believe in God and in Jesus, his Son.

Many Christians pray to Mary, the mother of Jesus, in heaven and ask her to pray to Jesus on their behalf.

Often, people say that they have received special answers to prayer after praying in the Holy House. Do you think this is because it is a holy place, the place where Mary appeared to Richeldis de Faverches, or could answers to prayer happen anywhere?

Activity 3: A reflective circle time

This activity is designed to help the children think about why some Christians use symbols such as water and candles to say their prayers, and why some places, such as the Holy House and well at Walsingham, are special.

Before the circle time begins, ask the children to look through magazines and newspapers for stories of sad and happy things that have happened to people, and cut them out. Ask them to bring the stories and place them in a pile in front of them on the floor when they sit in the circle.

Put an attractive cloth over a low table in the centre of the circle. Place a large, shallow, clear glass bowl of water on the cloth. Light a large candle next to the bowl.

Ask the children to sit very still and look at the items on the table. Ask them to share their thoughts about how these things make them feel. Invite them to suggest words that describe their feelings.

Talk about water and light as symbols for Christians. For example, baptism is a symbol for Christians of becoming part of God's family. Water is a symbol of refreshment and renewal and also a symbol for forgiveness and new life. The resurrection of Jesus is represented by a lit candle. The candle also reminds Christians that Jesus called himself 'the light of the world'.

Ask children to share some of the cuttings they have brought. Reflect together on the sad and happy things going on in the local community, in the family, the school and the world. Talk about how Christians tell God about these things in their prayers. Water and candles help Christians to focus on their thoughts when they are in special places like the Holy House at Walsingham, or in a church, or their own room at home. Have a discussion about whether a place to focus thoughts or prayers has to be a special, holy place.

End with a period of quiet. Suggest to the children that they may wish to offer their own thoughts silently as they look at the cuttings, the light and the water.

You may wish to have tealights available for the children to light individually and place near their cuttings. Alternatively, you could place floating candles in the water.

Holywell: St Winifred's Well

Teacher fact file

- St Winifred's Well is at Holywell in Flintshire. It is the most visited holy well in Britain.
- The well has been a shrine since the Middle Ages. It is dedicated to St Winifred.
- Legend has it that Winifred was murdered by a chieftain called Caradoc. He struck off her head, and where it fell, a spring arose that later became the well. The earth then opened and swallowed up Caradoc!
- Winifred's uncle, Beuno, who later became a saint himself, replaced her head on her shoulders and Winifred was restored to life!
- Henry VIII's grandmother, Margaret Beaufort, rebuilt the well in 1490. Because of this, he did not order it to be destroyed at the Reformation.
- Today the well is cared for by Roman Catholic nuns.
- People of all faiths visit the well and bathing pools nearby. The water is free and many people bring bottles with them to fill and take home. Local people often keep a bottle of the water in their homes to use in times of injury or distress. The water is believed to have healing powers.
- Traditionally, the well has always been a place of prayer, especially for women who are suffering from illness.

For resources and information about St Winifred's Well, telephone 01352 713054.

Focus

This is another example of a legend that reports miraculous events. The story of St Winifred gives an opportunity to discuss with the children the whole concept of what a legend is. Often legends contain unbelievable accounts of unbelievable events, just as this one appears to do! However, it is also an example of how belief or religious faith, and events which may or may not have happened exactly as it says in the story, can lead to a place becoming a famous and holy place of pilgrimage. It also illustrates how people today still visit such sites to pray for healing and refreshment in their lives.

The symbolic message of this shrine is that water is a symbol of healing and love. In the story, after the hatred and violence of the chieftain, Winifred was shown love and care by her uncle and was restored to life. At this well today, people remember those who suffer as a result of violence across the world, especially women.

Discussion starters

Ask the children to think about demonstrations of violence across the world, such as the 11 September 2001 attack, other terrorist attacks, wars and abuse. Talk about how it might help some people to offer thoughts and prayers in a special holy place such as St Winifred's Well.

Activity 1: Make a collage pool

Children may enjoy making a large pool using materials such as papier mâché, paints, shimmering blue and green fabric or shiny paper. The pool could then be displayed on a wall or placed in a corner of the classroom and used as a base for words or pictures associated with water as a symbol for Christians and people of other faiths.

Extend the activity by researching information about projects, such as WaterAid, that help people who suffer in the Third World because of a lack of water, or who do not have clean water supplies. Information gathered could also be placed on the pool.

Finally, the children could surround the pool with paper water droplet shapes on which they have drawn or written about why water is precious to them personally. For example, water is good to drink, to swim in or play in... and so on. The words 'I am thankful for water because...' could be printed on the droplets.

Activity 2: Come to the water!

The poem on Worksheet 6 (p. 85) could be read aloud by the class as a whole, presented as a dramatic recital or as a piece of choral speaking with percussion instruments in the background to enhance the atmosphere (especially tom-tom drums or instruments that produce a 'running water' sound effect), or simply used as a class reading activity.

Chester Cathedral: the Shrine of St Werburga

Teacher fact file

- St Werburga's Shrine was destroyed in the 1530s but has since been rebuilt. It is still a sacred place in Chester Cathedral and a focus for prayer and reflection.
- Medieval pilgrims flocked to Chester Cathedral to pray at her shrine, and a Benedictine abbey was established there which became extremely wealthy.
- This shrine became one of the busiest and most popular in the country.
- Werburga (or Werburgh as she is sometimes known) was a nun. She founded nunneries at Threekingham in Lincolnshire, Hanbury in Staffordshire and Weedon Bec in Northamptonshire.
- She died at Threekingham and her body was taken to Hanbury. It was later brought to Chester to keep it safe when the Danes invaded.
- Werburga was a powerful and respected leader in the church. She has become an example of equality in the church for men and women.
- Werburga's symbol is a pair of geese.

For resources and information about visits to St Werburga's Shrine, contact the Education Officer at Chester Cathedral.
Telephone 01244 500957.
E-mail: davies@chestercathedral.com, or visit the website at www.chestercathedral.com.

Activity 1: The legend of St Werburga

Here is a famous legend about St Werburga and the flock of geese that lived at Weedon Bec nunnery in Northamptonshire. The legend reminds people of St Werburga's leadership and sense of justice. It is a reminder too of the respect and authority that Werburga earned within the church during her life. It also offers an example of her healing powers and prayerfulness. All of these attributes can be explored with the children when talking about why Werburga became a saint and what it was that drew pilgrims to come to her shrine to pray.

This story is yet another example of a powerful legend associated with a saint and shrine. Yet, like many other saints, pilgrims came to pray to her because they had faith and belief in her as a holy servant of God, who would pray to Jesus for them in heaven and help them in their daily lives.

It was a warm, sunny day in Weedon Bec. Werburga and the other nuns were about to set to work in the gardens and the fields.

'Sister Clare, please go and weed the vegetable garden,' asked Werburga politely.

'Sister Julian, please check on the corn that is growing in the back field.'

'Yes, Mother Werburga,' answered Sister Julian.

They all set off to do their work. Werburga headed towards the rose garden to begin pruning the rose bushes. Suddenly, she heard a voice behind her. She turned around and saw Sister Julian running towards her.

'Mother, mother, come quickly! The geese have been eating the corn again!'

Werburga ran towards the corn field straight away.

'Oh no!' she exclaimed. 'Just look what they have done to our beautiful golden corn! It was almost ready for cutting! Look at it, they have chewed it right down to the stubble!'

Sister Julian ran to fetch some of the other sisters who were working nearby. Everyone stood looking at the corn field in disbelief.

'Something has to be done about these geese, sisters!' said Werburga. She stomped across the field, shouting as she went, 'Geese, geese, where are you? Come out of those bushes, I need to speak to you!'

A loud cackling sound rang out as first one, then two, then three, four, five, six geese waddled out from among the shrubs and bushes.

'What have you got to say for yourselves, you naughty geese?' said Werburga sternly.

The geese looked at her and began to cackle even louder.

'You can stop that dreadful noise!' she said angrily. 'Now listen to me, all of you.'

The geese stopped cackling and stood very still.

'You are all very greedy birds,' she told them. 'We feed you every day and give you fresh straw to sleep in. Why, then, have you eaten our corn? We need this to feed the cows through the winter!'

The geese hung their heads in shame.

'Greediness is a sin,' she went on. 'You should be thankful for the food you have each day and you should not go around eating everyone else's food as well!' she said, wagging her finger at them. 'I am very sorry, but there is no longer a home for you here. I want you to leave this place tomorrow morning.'

One of the elder geese looked up at Werburga. 'I am very sorry, Mother Werburga. We will leave early in the morning,' he said.

'Thank you,' she said politely and stomped back across the field.

That night, when all the sisters were in bed and the geese were curled up in their straw nest for the very last time, there was a rustling sound next to the bird house. Suddenly the door flew wide open and two men crept in. The geese awoke with a start. 'POACHERS!' yelled the elder goose with fear in his voice. The geese got up and began to run towards the open door. The poachers ran round and round, trying to grab each goose as it passed by.

'Got one!' shouted one of the men. He grabbed the goose by the neck and twisted hard with both hands. There was one last loud squawk before the goose died.

'Got yer!' said the poacher. 'Come on, men, that will have to do for one night. Let's get away before the ladies of the house wake up. Those geese are making such a noise out there!' The men ran away across the fields.

Early next morning, Werburga headed towards the bird house. There were feathers all over the ground. The elder of the geese was waiting for her at the door.

'Whatever has happened here?' she asked.

'Poachers, mother, during the night. One of our flock has been killed. I am afraid we cannot leave here now. We will not go!' said the elder goose.

Werburga covered her face with her hands. 'I shall investigate this matter straight away,' she said. 'These men must be caught!'

Werburga called together all the villagers and asked for their help in finding the poachers. It was not long before they brought the men to the nunnery. The thieves still had the goose and it had not yet been plucked ready to go in the cooking pot.

'Bring the goose to me,' Werburga said to the poacher who stood before her with it in his hands. 'Do you not know it is wrong to steal and to kill?'

Werburga took the goose to the bird house. She stroked it gently with her hands and whispered quiet words. Suddenly it began to lift up its head.

'He's come back to life!' shouted the elder goose. 'She's brought him back to life!'

The geese were so thankful to Werburga for bringing their brother goose back to life that they agreed straight away to leave Weedon Bec. Off they went to find a new home. From that day on, everyone realized that Werburga was a very special woman.

Activity 2: Looking at modern religious communities

Leading on from this story and the brief glimpse of Werburga's life, the children could investigate modern religious communities, in particular those for women who feel called to life as a nun. Follow the research with a discussion about the whole concept of vocation.

Anglican communities who can offer further information/resources are:

For women:
Community of St Clare, St Mary's Convent, Freeland, Witney, Oxon. Tel: 01993 881225
Order of the Holy Paraclete, St Hilda's Priory, Sneaton Castle, Whitby, N. Yorks. Tel: 01947 602079
The Society of St Margaret, The Priory of Our Lady of Walsingham. Tel: 01328 820340
Community of the Holy Name, Derby. Tel: 01332 671716
Community of All Hallows, Ditchingham, Norfolk. Tel: 01986 892749

For men:
Community of the Resurrection, Mirfield, Yorkshire. Tel: 01924 494318
Society of St Francis, Hilfield. Tel: 01300 341345. E-mail: ssf.orders.anglican.org
Benedictine Community, Elmore Abbey, Newbury, Berks. Tel: 01635 33080

Activity 3: Goosey! Goosey!

This activity is based on a traditional English craft. Give each child a copy of Worksheet 7 (p. 86). Ask the children to cut out the goose and to make at least ten copies of the feather.

Ask the children to write the words in the frame on the feathers. Have a discussion about the words on the feathers and what they mean for the world, for different nations, or for Christians today. Discuss how the story and life of St Werburga illustrates these words. What other words might the children wish to include? Write these words on the blank feathers.

Invite the children to decorate the edges of the feathers and the goose's head (using coloured crayons) with pictures that remind them of the words. Glue the feathers to the goose's body. Punch a hanging hole in the finished goose and use thread to hang each goose as a display, or use several geese to make a mobile.

Lincoln Cathedral: the Shrine of St Hugh

Teacher fact file

- St Hugh was born in Burgundy, France in 1135.
- He became a monk in the Carthusian order and was appointed procurator of their headquarters in France.
- He became a scholar and was a gentle but assertive man.
- In 1178, King Henry II founded the first Carthusian monastery in Witham, Somerset, as an act of contrition for the murder of Thomas à Becket. He appointed Hugh as prior there.
- Hugh made his mark from the start by refusing to move in to the monastery until the king had built homes for the villagers.
- He became Bishop of Lincoln in 1186. He built a new cathedral there and raised the low morale of the city. He also re-founded schools.
- Hugh stood up for the poor who were in danger of starvation as a result of the royal hunting and forestry laws that had been imposed after the Norman Conquest. Hugh refused to accept them.
- Hugh showed great bravery in his life. He offered sanctuary to the Jews who lived in Lincoln when Richard I came to the throne. Rioters threatened the lives of the Jews and Hugh confronted the troublemakers personally. He did the same thing in Northampton and saved the lives of many Jews there.
- Hugh travelled widely across his diocese throughout his life and loved to spend time with children and animals.
- He died in 1200 and was buried in the Angel Choir of his Cathedral.
- The Pope made Hugh a saint in 1220.
- St Hugh's great tomb soon became a shrine for pilgrims who came to pray to him there. It became the second largest shrine in the country next to Canterbury.
- His tomb is still a place of peaceful prayer in Lincoln Cathedral. Today people can stop there and remember or pray for those who are persecuted because of their race, as well as those who are poor and weak in society.
- St Hugh's symbols are a swan, because Hugh kept a pet swan at his Manor at Stow, and a chalice with the infant Jesus on it.

For resources and information about visits to Lincoln Cathedral, contact the Education Department at Lincoln Cathedral.
E-mail: education@lincolncathedral.com.

Activity 1: Fact files

Talk to the children about the life of St Hugh, based on the information on page 45. Using Worksheet 8 (p. 87), the children could then produce their own fact file about him, picking out key words to describe his character and the example he set in his life.

Activity 2: What would you do?

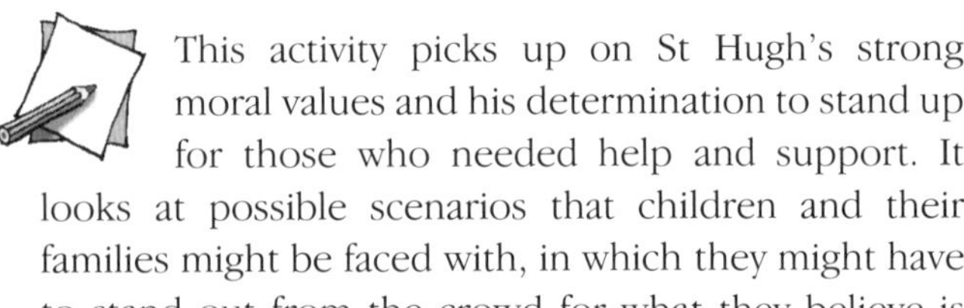

This activity picks up on St Hugh's strong moral values and his determination to stand up for those who needed help and support. It looks at possible scenarios that children and their families might be faced with, in which they might have to stand out from the crowd for what they believe is right. The scenarios are set out on Worksheet 9 (p. 88).

The children debate the questions, then vote for their answers. They may also wish to come up with their own scenarios for debate. They could work in small groups on each scenario, with each group taking turns to present and run the class debate.

Activity 3: Standing up for human rights

The wider subject of human rights could be explored with the children—for example, the Holocaust in World War II, apartheid in South Africa, the massacres in Rwanda more recently, and other places where people have been persecuted and killed because of their religious faith.

With younger children, simply reading stories or watching videos about children or families from other cultures—in particular the diary of Anne Frank, available in more simplified formats—can raise awareness about people sharing communities with those from different cultures or religious backgrounds.

Famous people who have stood up for human rights and risked or lost their own lives, such as Martin Luther King, Bishop Trevor Huddleston and Nelson Mandela, could also be explored and compared to St Hugh.

Bury St Edmunds, Suffolk: the Shrine of St Edmund

Teacher fact file

- Edmund was born in 841. He was a devout Christian and later became king of East Anglia.
- When the Danes invaded, monasteries, abbeys and churches were destroyed all over the country.
- In 870, Edmund gathered forces together to fight the Danes. He was captured after fighting a terrible battle but he refused to give up his faith or to swear allegiance to the Danes.
- He was tied to a tree at Hoxne in Suffolk, and was subsequently shot with arrows. When he was almost dead, they cut off his head.
- Legend tells us that his head was cast into a nearby forest, then the Danes left it there and impaled his body on the tree. Edmund's followers took down the body and some of them recovered Edmund's head from the forest. The legend says that they found it resting between the paws of a wolf, who gave it up to them straight away. The head was placed back on the body and no one could tell that it had been cut off, so the story says!
- Edmund's body was buried at Hoxne and the tree remained alive there until 1848. There is now a monument there to mark where it stood.
- In 903, Edmund's body was moved to Bury St Edmunds. Monks began building the abbey there in 925 and Edmund's tomb became a shrine. Many pilgrims, including kings and queens, came to venerate him and pray there.

For resources and information about school visits to St Edmundsbury Cathedral, contact the Education Officer, The Discovery Centre, Angel Hill, Bury St Edmunds, Suffolk.
Telephone: Cathedral Office 01284 754933.
Website: www.stedscathedral.co.uk/discovery.htm.

Yet again there is a legendary focus to this story, but like the stories of many of the other saints in this book, we read of a man who showed bravery, stood up for his Christian faith and was prepared to die for what he believed in. As a result the Church made him a saint.

In 1215, the Magna Carta was drawn up at St Edmund's shrine and King John swore on St Edmund's bones to abide by the document. Today, all that remains are ruins of the great abbey and monastery, but there is a new shrine to St Edmund in the cathedral on the adjoining site.

It may be best to tell the story of what happened to St Edmund in your own words, in appropriate detail for your children, because it's quite a gruesome story. Once the story has been told, the children can then be encouraged to explore what happened to St Edmund and why he sacrificed his life for his Christian faith, through the following activities.

Activity 1: Only a tree

This activity is a dramatized reading, but could also be performed as a dance drama. It requires imagination, and looks at the legend from the point of view of the tree on which Edmund died.

If desired, the children could compose a dance to depict the soldiers, followers and other trees in the forest. Discuss with the children suitable music to accompany different parts of the drama.

Based on this story, comparisons can be made with the death of Jesus on a cross of wood that was once a tree. There is much scope for discussion here.

CAST

- ★ Tree trunk
- ★ Branch 1
- ★ Branch 2
- ★ Branch 3
- ★ Branch 4
- ★ Leaf 1
- ★ Leaf 2

Tree trunk: I am only a tree. I stand tall and wide. I have grown and stretched towards the sky for many a year. Who cares about me? I am only a tree.

Branch 1: I spread my hands out broad and long near the earth to keep this tree standing strong. Against the winds and rain and snow, it needs my support. So I bend low above the earth. I am this big old tree's best friend.

Branch 2: I am the middle man—yes, that's me! When you look at this tree, it's me you see! I am at eye level and I see life! The birds and the squirrels all hop up on me!

Branch 3: I'm right up here, look... up here am I. The tree needs me to keep him steady at the top, so I need a good head for heights! No good getting dizzy when the March winds blow! I need to know which way to go.

Branch 4: And I'm the branch that saw them first, the day that Edmund's horse came by! I sensed the danger all around. I wanted to reach out and pull him up! Too late! The soldiers were there as Edmund stood against the tree.

Branch 2: I'm the one who felt it first! The rope pulled tight around me when they tied him to this tree. I could not move. I felt my bark begin to crackle and burst as the rope pulled tighter still.

Branch 1: I shouted and swayed and stretched and pulled, but the soldiers only stood on me. I felt their weight. I almost snapped. But then they stopped and all went still.

Branch 3: I saw it first when the bag came out—the bag of arrows tall and stout. And one by one they pulled them out. I saw them glisten in the sun! I looked to the sky and said a prayer when the bow-string stretched and squeaked.

Tree trunk: It seemed like a lifetime waiting for what we knew would fly. I pulled my wood, my sap, my bark so tight, I thought that I would burst.

Leaf 1: I am the leaf that slowly fell when the arrow flew from out of the bow. I could not help, or warn, or tell that his life and mine were over now.

Leaf 2: I lost my grip as arrows flew, now sharply, quickly, one by one. I fluttered down and landed on his arm. I heard him make a crying sound, but then I floated to the ground.

Branch 3: I saw the sword shine in the sun as the soldier drew it from his waist. I tried to look towards the sky as down it came upon his head.

Tree trunk: We held him there, this man of faith. It's all that we could do for him. We held him till his friends arrived. They took him down and it was done.

Branch 1: We stood and grew for many a year. As each branch grew, we told the story of Edmund who, just like Jesus, died on a tree.

Tree trunk: Remember him, for he was brave so long ago. Perhaps one day to his shrine you'll go?

Activity 2: Leaves

Using brown sugar paper or thin card, make a wall display of a large tree, similar to the one in the drawing on this page. Photocopy the leaf shape on to thin card to provide each child with a leaf template. Ask the children to make paper leaf shapes using the template.

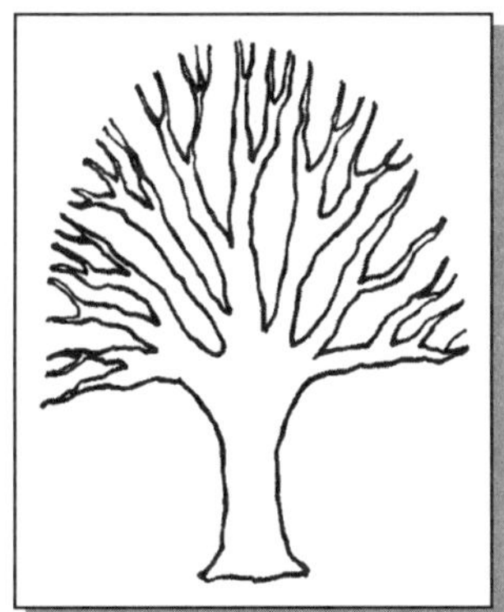

They can then write words on their leaf shapes that represent what Edmund did in standing up for his beliefs.

The children can also write, on other leaves, words or sentences to illustrate how modern-day people (adults or children) may have to stand up to situations, or to suffering and difficulties. The leaves can then be coloured and stuck on the tree to make a class display.

Some children may wish to make this a prayer tree by writing little prayers on the leaves for people who have to stand up to difficult situations.

Activity 3: Design a monument

There is a monument standing in Hoxne, where the tree that Edmund died on used to be. What sort of monument would the children design to mark this spot? Would it be made of wood or stone? What words, illustrations or symbols would they put on it?

Discussion could take place about the fact that this story is a 'legend'. What about the wolf who held Edmund's head? Could this part of the story be true? Would the children wish the wolf to be remembered on the monument, or should the wolf have a memorial place too?

Like the tree, the wolf represents how 'nature' held Edmund in his time of pain and death. This could be discussed with older children.

What about Edmund's followers? Remember how they took care of his body after he had died. Should they have a monument of their own?

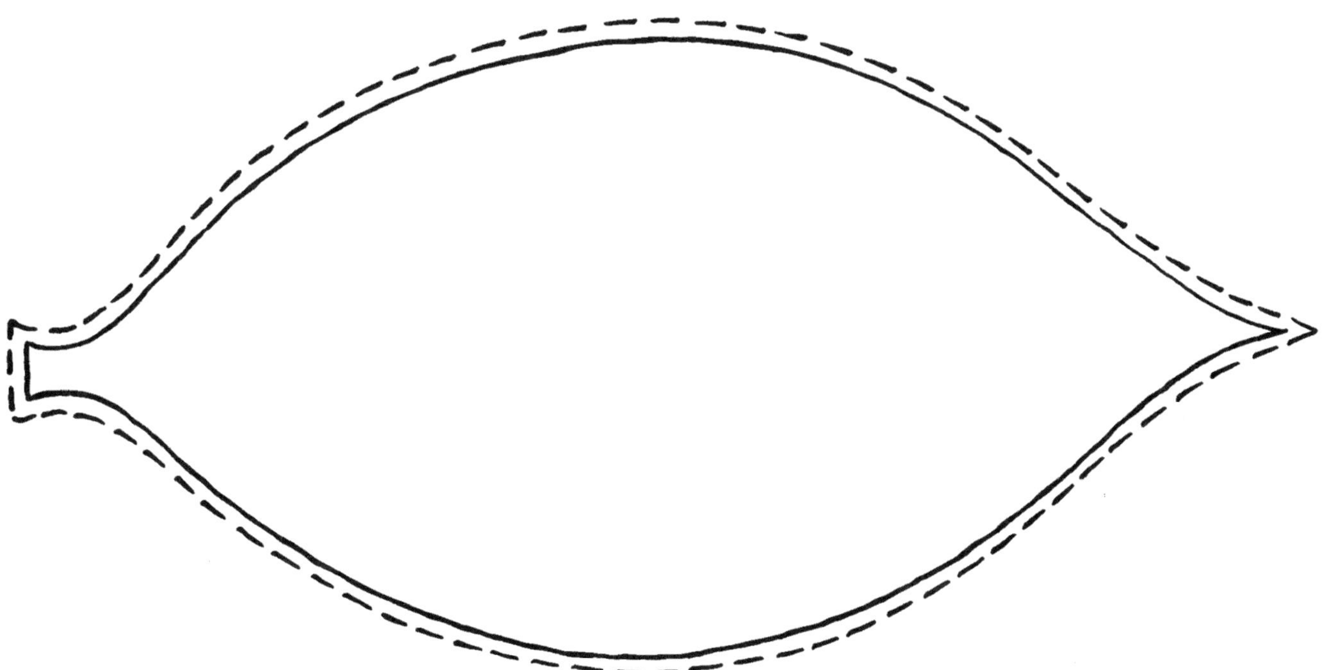

The Island of Iona, Scotland: St Columba

Teacher fact file

- St Columba landed on Iona in the year 563. Before this, he was a monk in Ireland and founded many monasteries there.
- Columba sailed to Iona to build a new life there, along with twelve companions.
- No one is sure what his reasons were for going to Iona. Maybe it was 'voluntary exile for Christ', or to help overseas compatriots in their struggle for survival, or maybe he was exiled as a punishment for causing a bloody battle between monasteries over a psalter he had copied but refused to give up. Many lives were lost in the battle.
- As a priest and monk, he founded a community on the island. He was given money to do so by the ruler of the Irish kingdom of Dalriada.
- Columba loved nature, for it expressed to him the love of God the Creator.
- Columba died in 567. On Iona today, the mound of Columba's cell can be found, along with the site of his tomb.
- Columba did much to spread the Christian faith in Scotland and travelled widely.
- He was a great scribe and poet. He was also an artist and illuminated texts.
- His relics were taken to Dunkeld in 849 after Viking raids on Iona, and pilgrims came to venerate them at his shrine there.
- Iona Cathedral was restored in the early 1900s by the Duke of Argyle.
- The new Iona community was founded in 1938 by the Very Revd Lord Macleod of Fuinary. It is a place of prayer, pilgrimage and retreat for both Catholics and Protestants. It is possible to arrange pilgrimages around the island.

For resources and information about visits to Iona (including pilgrimages around the island), contact the Iona Community. Telephone 0141 332 6343, or visit their website at www.iona.org.uk.

Activity 1: Columba and the weary crane

After telling the children a little about Columba, the following short play based on legends about him could be read, either in small groups or by the class as a whole. Discussion could then take place about which aspects of Columba's personality and work as a Christian and as a saint are illustrated in the stories. They are adapted from the writings on the life of St Columba by St Adamnan, and the writings of Curtayne.

CAST

★ Columba
★ Monk
★ Narrator

Narrator: One day, in the Abbey on Iona, Columba called one of his monks to his cell. He asked him to come and look out of the window.

Columba: Brother, in three days' time I want you to go to the hilltop over there and wait on the beach.

Monk: But it is a long walk, brother!

Columba: I want you to wait on the beach because when the third hour before sunset is passed, a crane will come flying in from the northern coasts. She will be very tired and hurt by the wind. She will fall on the beach at your feet. Pick her up carefully and carry her to a shelter nearby. Be kind to her and feed her for three days and nights. Take her back then to the beach and let her go, so that she can fly back again to the old sweet land of Ireland where she came from. This is the land where you and I also grew up.

Monk: I will do as you command, brother.

Narrator: The monk did as he was told and everything happened just as Columba had said it would. When the monk returned to the monastery, he went straight in to tell Columba all about it.

Monk: Brother, the crane arrived just as you said and now she is on her way again!

Columba: May God bless you, my son, for you have cared for this pilgrim visitor. When three suns have set, she will be back in her own land.

Narrator: And so it happened.

Activity 2: St Columba and the sad child

Read out this story as a class or group.

One day, Columba set off on a journey to visit the Picts on the mainland of Scotland. He wanted to tell them stories from the New Testament in the Bible about Jesus. On his way, he met a ruler of the Picts who was not a Christian. He was a druid.

Columba stopped to say hello. Suddenly he saw a little girl standing nearby. She was very thin and she had a white face.

'She looks like a ghost!' said Columba. 'Who is this child and why does she look so sad?' he asked.

'She is only a slave from Ireland. What does it matter as long as she does her scrubbing and sweeping?' said the ruler.

Columba felt troubled. 'Please let this little girl go free!' he said to the man. 'I will then see that she gets home safely to Ireland.'

'No, I will not!' he replied.

Columba went on his way. He could not stop thinking about the sad little girl.

After a while, the ruler became very ill. He wrote down a message and sent it to Columba in Iona.

'Please help me. I need a cure,' the letter said.

When Columba read the message, he sent a letter back to the ruler. 'I will make you well again if you let the little girl go,' he wrote.

The ruler was very angry. 'Why is he so worried about this little good-for-nothing girl?' he shouted. 'Go and tell him I will not let her go free!' he said to his messenger.

As soon as the messenger had left to go back to Iona, the ruler got much worse. He was rolling around in his bed in pain. 'I think I am going to die!' he yelled.

He called another messenger to him. 'Go

quickly to Columba. Tell him I will let the little girl go free. But he must come and help me!' he said.

Columba did not trust the Pict ruler. He sent two of his monks to fetch the little girl. As soon as he knew she was safe, he set sail from Iona and went to the man's house. He cured him of his illness.

Activity 3: A Celtic prayer

Prayers in the Celtic Christian tradition are often based on nature and creation. St Columba himself used nature to teach about God and his love for all of creation. The prayer on Worksheet 10 (p. 89) is a good example of a Celtic Christian prayer. Children may design their own illuminated letter at the start of it. They could then add further lines to the prayer, beginning with the words, 'Deep peace...' They may also enjoy creating individual pictures or a group mural using paint, pastels or collage to depict the words of the prayer.

As a follow-up, the children could also try writing their own prayer in the Celtic style with an emphasis on nature.

Discussion starters

Follow the prayer writing activity with a discussion about the ways in which the beauty of nature might help Christians today to feel closer to God. Many Christians today enjoy going to the beautiful island of Iona on pilgrimages and holidays, to pray in the church there and walk in the countryside and on the beaches. Why do the children think that this is so?

Pose the question: 'Do holy or sacred spaces have to be shrines or churches? Can they just be beautiful, peaceful places?' This takes the children back to where they began when considering their own special places in the introductory section of this book.

Activity 4: A stilling activity

Use an interesting and fairly large seashell as a focus to tell this visualization story to the class. Follow the activity by inviting the children to complete the story in their own words, or to write a poem about the shell's adventures. What happened next to the shell? How did it eventually end up in the classroom?

Start by showing the children the shell and giving them these instructions: 'Close your eyes and sit comfortably... Breathe in and out very deeply and slowly three times... Now listen very carefully. Try to picture in your mind everything that is happening in the story I am going to read to you.'

Now read the story slowly, pausing as indicated.

Here I am at the end of my journey... I have travelled very far to be here today... Look at me... How old am I? I have been smoothed by the wind and waves... I have been tossed about and turned around... Once, a little creature lived inside me... but that was a long while ago... I sat at the bottom of the deep, deep ocean... It was dark and cold... I was never alone, though. I had jellyfish, octopi and beautiful coral to keep me company...

One day, a huge fish who was searching for food swam by... He flipped me over with his tail. He woke me up from my morning nap. I felt myself rising... up... and up... and up... in the dark, murky water... Suddenly I was being thrown around and the waves whooshed around my fragile back... I felt as though I would crack in two... Then suddenly I landed... I could feel the soft, wet sand underneath me... I was safe! ...

There are instructions about how to introduce 'stilling' and lots of ideas for using the technique with children in the book *Don't Just Do Something—Sit There* by Mary Stone (RMEP, 1995).

Activity 5: Design a Celtic cross

The ancient geometrical and interlaced knot and circle pattern is a distinct feature of the Celtic cross. The children can use Worksheet 11 (p. 90) to study the knot and circle design of a typical Celtic cross and then create their own design in the template provided.

BRF have published a useful resource book full of information about crosses from around the world, including the Celtic cross. *A-cross the World*, by Martyn Payne and Betty Pedley, is available direct from BRF, or from Christian bookshops, priced £15.99.

Westminster Abbey, London: the Shrine of St Edward

Teacher fact file

- This magnificent cathedral houses two very different sacred sites: the Shrine of St Edward the Confessor and the Tomb of the Unknown Warrior.
- St Edward's shrine was once adorned with gold and jewels and venerated by pilgrims. It was stripped bare at the Reformation and his bones were removed. Queen Mary reinstated the bones and rebuilt the shrine. She also restored the abbey as a monastery.
- Edward the Confessor, the last Saxon king of England, died in 1066. He worked for peace in the country throughout his life, was a man of prayer and was generous to the poor.
- It is reported that he experienced visions and cured people of an illness called scrofula (the king's evil). People viewed him as a holy man.
- It is thought that he may have founded the abbey, and historical records show that he built the palace of Westminster.

For resources and information about visits to Westminster Abbey, telephone 0207 2225152 or e-mail: info@westminster-abbey.org.

Activity 1: The legend of St Edward's ring

Here is a famous story about St Edward the Confessor.

One day, King Edward saw a poor beggar in Westminster. 'Stop! Stop this carriage!' he shouted to his footman. The horses snorted as their reins were pulled tightly and the king's carriage came to a sudden halt.

'Bring that poor man over to me!' said the king. His footman climbed down from the carriage and went over to where the beggar was sitting at the side of the road.

'The king wants you. Come with me,' he said.

The beggar was shocked. When he got to the carriage, the king reached a hand out of the window.

'This is for you, my man,' he said, holding out a shiny gold ring. 'Now move on!' he shouted to the footman.

The beggar stared at the ring that had been placed in his hand by the king. He did not even have time to say 'thank you'.

Two years later, two English pilgrims were on pilgrimage in the Holy Land. One day, while walking along a road, they met a man. 'Hello,' they said. 'Are you a pilgrim, like us?'

'I am St John the apostle, one of Jesus' disciples,' said the man. 'I want you to take this ring back to King Edward. Please warn him that his life may be in danger in six months' time!' And he placed the king's ring in the hand of one of the pilgrims.

ADAPTED FROM THE ACCOUNT IN THE *OXFORD DICTIONARY OF SAINTS* FIFTH EDITION (OXFORD UNIVERSITY PRESS, 2004).

We do not know how this strange story ended, but many churches across England have reference to it. For example, a church in Ludlow, Shropshire, has a stained-glass window that shows pictures of it. There is a window depicting the story in York Minster, and, in Westminster Abbey itself, there are some tiles with pictures of the story on them.

As a follow-up to the story, the children might like to create a storyboard of the events or try drawing what they think the ring might have looked like.

Activity 2: Creating a stained-glass window of the story

Provide each child with an A4 piece of cellophane or OHP acetate and ask them to design a stained-glass window picture depicting the story, using stained-glass felt pens or paints. The finished work can then be displayed on the windows of the classroom.

Use real ceramic tiles or make squares from thick cardboard or vinyl and ask the children to design a tile that depicts the story, or ask them to design a symbol to represent St Edward the Confessor, using acrylic paints, stained-glass paints or pens. Alternatively, for older children, the tiles could be produced first on paper, then remade using coloured felt pieces and stuck on to squares of cardboard.

Westminster Abbey, London: the Tomb of the Unknown Warrior

Teacher fact file

- The tomb of the Unknown Warrior is situated in the nave of the cathedral. An unidentified soldier from World War I is buried there.
- The tomb was placed there among the splendid tombs and memorials of many rich and powerful people in order to draw attention to the great sacrifice made by so many young men for their country, whatever their class or rank.
- It is a place where visitors to the cathedral can stand quietly and think or pray about the sacrifices made by ordinary men and women in conflicts across the world, and those losing their lives in conflicts today.

For resources and information about visits to Westminster Abbey, telephone 0207 2225152 or e-mail: info@westminster-abbey.org.

Activity 1: He has no name

The following poem is based on the story of the Tomb of the Unknown Warrior. It can either be read aloud to the children or performed by the children in pairs, small groups or as a whole-class presentation.

The poem aims to help the children think about who this man might have been and why he is remembered in this way.

Voices, footsteps heard each day
Some don't look, they just pass by.
Clicking cameras, finding tombs,
Glancing at watches, hurrying on.

A ring of poppies marks the spot,
Their petals red like the blood he shed.
He has no name, but he was brave
And died that day in France.

Some voices stop and feet stand still
Upon the polished marble spot.
They think of wars in days gone by
And fighting that goes on today.

He has no name so we don't know
Who he was, rich or poor,
Or what he'd say about that day,
He died for king and country.

Using Worksheet 12 (p. 91), ask the children to design symbols that illustrate the theme of the poem, after they have read and discussed it. They can then create a border to decorate the poem with these symbols.

Discussion starters

The poem may spark discussion about present-day conflicts across the world, and thoughts about those who give their lives to bring peace and freedom in various places across the world.

Discuss with the children whether they think that a simple memorial like this in a cathedral might help people to think or pray. In what ways is this tomb the same as or different from a shrine such as the shrine of St Edward?

Activity 2: Creative writing

Encourage the children to write a story about the unknown warrior and try to imagine who he was.

Activity 3: Designing a sacred space

Ask the children to think about what kind of memorial they would put in Westminster Abbey, or in a church or special building, to help people to think or pray.

Follow this discussion by talking about how they might design a special garden, or a thinking or prayer spot to go in their school playground, hall or classroom. In what ways could this be a place for children and teachers to be still and quiet? They may wish to conduct a survey around the school to see if others would welcome such a spot. There is lots of room for discussion and further work on this project!

SECTION 3

Pilgrimage in the Bible

Part 1

The story of Noah

Bible reference
Genesis 6:1—9:17

Teacher fact file

- This story may be found in the Old Testament book of Genesis. It tells of a journey of faith that is very different from the stories that have been explored in this book so far.
- It tells how God chose Noah and his family to be the only people who were saved when a great flood came upon earth.
- Noah was given responsibility for ensuring that a male and female of each species of creature were gathered into a boat—the ark that God had asked him to build.
- Noah trusted God and agreed to follow his instructions and do what God asked of him. He showed great faith and led his whole family to do likewise.
- Noah and his family were asked to trust, obey and set off on a voyage, not knowing where they would end up or what the future would hold.
- The story offers an example of people who were prepared to put their lives totally into the hands of God.
- Children can explore similarities and contrasts to the material in Sections 1 and 2.
- For Jews and Christians, it is important to read these stories in their holy books, as they show how God has been involved with the whole of his creation right from the beginning. He provides his people with a beautiful world that holds within it all they need to live.
- This story also reminds Christians that God's people are very precious to him and it saddens him if they do not respect one another and the world they live in. This theme continues throughout the Old and New Testaments of the Bible.

Activity 1: Harry and the storm

This contemporary story is designed to introduce the story of Noah to the children. It is ideal for reading aloud, or as a paired reading activity in class.

Harry sat in his shed at the bottom of the garden. He was in a bad mood.

'Holidays are boring!' he said to himself as he sat staring at the rain-streaked window pane. Harry's two best friends, John and Carl, had both gone away on holidays with their families, but Harry's parents had to work through the Easter holidays so here he was at home, fed up and bored—*and* it was raining!

The rain was not the only reason Harry felt miserable. At lunch time he had had an argument with his mum. Harry's bedroom was a real mess and his mum had told him off about it. After lunch, he had run out of the house to the bottom of the garden and into the old garden shed, which stood half-hidden behind the bushes. Harry's mum always let him use the shed as a playhouse.

'I can make as much mess as I like in here!' he said angrily to himself, slamming the door behind him.

Now the rain was pouring down outside. Harry jumped suddenly as he heard a loud crack of thunder and the sky lit up with lightning. He felt scared.

'I'm not going indoors, though!' he said stubbornly out loud.

Harry wiped the steamy window pane with his hands. It was becoming very dark outside and Harry saw his mum switch on the kitchen light. Then the kitchen door opened and he could see his mum standing in the doorway. He could just about hear her voice.

'Harry, come on in!' she yelled. 'It's wild out there.'

He pretended not to hear her and put his hands over both ears defiantly.

Mum was worried, so she grabbed her old raincoat off the peg on the back of the kitchen door, flung it over her head and made a dash down the garden path. She ran so quickly that when she reached the shed door it shot open and she almost fell inside.

'There you are, you silly boy!' she exclaimed. 'You must be freezing out here. Why don't you come back to the house?'

Harry looked up and smiled. 'Mum, you're soaked!' he said with a giggle.

Mum laughed out loud. 'Move up!' she said, and plonked herself down on the wooden bench seat that Harry was sitting on.

'It's quite snug and warm, isn't it?' she said. 'No wonder you like to hide out down here. We'd better both wait here now until this dreadful storm comes to an end,' she added.

'I hate the rain,' said Harry in a grumpy voice.

'I know,' said Mum, 'but where would we be without it? It's a great gift, you know.' Then she started to smile.

'You know what? I feel just like Mrs Noah sitting here—you know, Noah's wife in that Bible story about Noah and the ark,' she added.

'Well, if this rain doesn't stop soon, we might have to build an ark, Mum!' exclaimed Harry.

'I used to love that story when I was a little girl,' Mum continued. 'I expect Noah and his family felt just like us when the rain started to fall. They had no idea when it was going to stop. It must have been really scary.'

Just then, there was another loud crack of thunder that made them both jump.

'I can't remember much about the story, actually,' said Harry.

'Well, let's remind ourselves,' said Mum. 'It'll take our minds off this storm.'

Mum began to tell the story. 'It all began when God got very upset and angry with the people on earth. They were behaving really badly.'

'You mean they didn't tidy their bedrooms, either?' asked Harry with a grin on his face.

'Oh, more than that. The story in Genesis tells us that they were treating each other really violently and planning many wicked, evil things. God felt very let down by them so he made a very difficult decision. He decided that the time had come to start again.

'God had his eye on Noah, though. He knew that Noah was a good man who was really trying his best, so he decided to choose him and all his family to do a special job for him. God often does that, you know—he chooses people out of the blue to do special things for him.' She paused for a moment to stretch out her legs, then she continued.

'God explained everything to Noah one day. He told him that he was planning to send enough rain to flood the whole world. He told Noah to get some wood and build an enormous boat—an ark. He told him the exact measurements, and that he should make rooms in it so that all the family could live on board. "You'll be safe, Noah, and all your family too," God told him. He promised Noah that all would be well.'

At this point Mum started to giggle.

'What's so funny?' asked Harry.

'Well I was just thinking... I don't know what I'd have said if I'd been Mrs Noah. Imagine Noah coming home for his tea and telling her she has to get everything packed up, get stacks of food together and sail away from everything she knows! I bet she must have thought he'd gone potty!'

'I bet she did, Mum. But didn't they have to get loads of animals together too?' asked Harry.

'That's right. God told Noah to gather a male and female of every species of creature on earth and put them on board the boat as well. Imagine it, climbing on board with all those smelly animals, birds and reptiles!' said Mum.

'Well, didn't Noah think it was all a bit strange?' asked Harry thoughtfully.

'That's the point. You see, the story says that Noah just did it. He *trusted* God. No questions asked, he just got on with it. It's a good job he did too, because it wasn't long before the rain began to fall and they all knew God really meant what he had said. The earth did begin to flood!'

'I think I know how they all felt. I've been in here for ages and the rain still hasn't stopped!' said Harry.

'Well, it rained for a bit longer than this in the story, Harry,' Mum continued. 'It rained for 40 whole days in the story! Soon the boat rose on the waters above the highest mountain tops. Every living thing on earth was destroyed. The Bible tells us that it then took another 150 days before the water started going down again.'

'Wow!' said Harry.

'Eventually the boat came to rest on a mountain called Ararat, and 40 days later Noah opened a window and sent out a raven,' explained Mum.

'Oh, we saw some ravens at the Tower of London last summer, didn't we?' exclaimed Harry.

'We did,' said Mum. 'But in the Bible story the raven just kept flying around, so Noah sent out a dove. But it could not find a place to land, so it flew back to Noah. Seven days later he sent it out again, and this time it came back with a green leaf from an olive tree in its beak.'

'So that must have meant there were trees beginning to grow again,' said Harry.

'That's right, and seven days after that Noah sent the dove out again. This time, the dove did not come back, so it must have found dry land to rest on.'

'I hope we aren't going to be stuck in here all that time, waiting for the rain to stop!' exclaimed Harry.

'Oh, but Noah and his family still had to be patient after this, until the land was dry enough to walk on. God told Noah when it was safe to leave the boat. He told Noah to let all the creatures go free so that they could find homes and start to breed.'

'I bet Noah and his family couldn't wait to get a proper house built after being squashed into that boat for so long!' said Harry.

'Well, the Bible tells us that first of all, before doing anything else, Noah said "thank you" to God. He built an altar and sacrificed an animal on it. That is what they did in those days to honour and worship God. God promised Noah that never again would such a terrible thing happen and that the whole family would be greatly blessed and have many children in the years to come.'

'Mum, look! Look outside! It's almost stopped raining. The rain is stopping at last!' shouted Harry.

'I do believe it is, Harry. You know, we have a lot to be thankful for, don't we?'

Mum opened the shed door. 'Hmm... have a sniff out here, Harry,' she said. They both poked their noses outside into the fresh, cool air.

'It smells all fresh and new. I can smell the leaves and flowers and grass. The rain has made everything new again. We are so lucky to have all these beautiful things, but we take them all for granted most of the time, don't we?'

'I suppose we do,' said Harry and, as he spoke, he looked up into the sky. 'Mum, look!' he yelled excitedly. 'Up there—it's a rainbow!'

They both gazed at the perfect rainbow in the sky.

'It's amazing, Harry, because that is just what happened at the end of the Noah story. I almost forgot. God placed a rainbow in the sky when they had all left the ark. He told Noah that the rainbow was a sign to them and to all people that he would keep his promise and that a flood like that would never happen again. That's why I love rainbows, Harry,' she said. 'They remind me that there is always hope, always a second chance, just like the sunshine that beams down again after a storm.'

'Sorry my room got in such a mess,' said Harry suddenly. Mum just smiled and gave him a hug.

'Come on, Mum, I'll race you to the house! It must be nearly teatime, I'm starving!' yelled Harry. And they both ran up the garden path.

Discussion starters

Noah trusted God because he believed in him. He was willing to set off into the unknown, leaving his home, because he trusted that God would keep his promise.

Discuss with the children times when they have had to trust, without knowing what was going to happen.

Noah and his family must have had to work as a team. There must have been difficulties and arguments. Harry and his mum had an argument, which affected their relationship with each other, but this was soon forgotten and forgiven. Is this important in our relationships with others? What if a family member, a team member or a friend behaves badly or lets us down? How should we deal with it?

Activity 2: Read it in the Bible

The children might like to read the story of Noah in the Contemporary English Version of the Bible.

Activity 3: Trusting one another

In pairs, the children take turns to be blindfolded and given instructions by their partner to get to different parts of the classroom or school hall. How easy or difficult is this?

How important is it to trust and to keep promises in everyday life? Other team games involving working together, trusting, or helping one another could be played to further illustrate the point.

Activity 4: Noah's 'pilgrimage'

God asked Noah to set off on a very different sort of pilgrimage. He did not know where his destination would be or how long the journey would take, but he knew that it was a journey he *must* make for God.

Noah and his family were asked to leave their homes and friends and the way of life they knew. Noah was willing to serve God and obey him without question. Do the children think this is a difficult, or even impossible, thing to do?

Compare the story of Noah with the stories of some of the pilgrims in Section 2. Can the children think of modern-day examples of people who have shown total obedience in what they have been asked to do, in the same way that Noah showed obedience to God?

A link could be made here to the life of Jesus and to Jesus' obedience to God. In what ways is Jesus' story similar to Noah's? In what ways is it different?

Activity 5: Make a trust chain

Give each child some paper-chain strips. Ask the children to write on the strips the names of people they trust and people who trust them (one name per strip). If there is room on the chain, they can also draw or write in what capacity they trust that person or are trusted by them. Discuss together situations when it is difficult to trust.

When the children have finished writing names on the strips, they could join all the strips together to make a long trust chain and hang it up in the classroom.

Activity 6: Rainbow messages

Photocopy the rainbow from Worksheet 13 (p. 92) and give each child their own copy. Ask the children to colour in a small part of each section of the rainbow with the appropriate colour. (Give them the order of colours—red, orange, yellow, green, blue, indigo, violet.)

When they have coloured each section, discuss with them what each colour might represent about life. After the discussion, ask them to write words or phrases that express what that colour represents about life for them personally. The aim is to create a rainbow that helps the children think about caring for others, trusting others and respecting creation.

When they have finished writing, they can continue to colour the sections around the words in the appropriate colour. Some children may wish to make a prayer rainbow, with each colour reminding them of a subject for prayer.

The story of Moses

Bible reference
Exodus 2:1—14:31

Teacher fact file

- This story is found in the Old Testament book of Exodus. It is a reminder yet again that God often chooses individuals to change course in their lives and to do things for him.
- This story is also a reminder that often the people God chooses are not rich, famous, intelligent or physically strong. They are people who have faith and are prepared to commit their lives to God and make great sacrifices for him.
- We meet Moses as a young man when he receives his call from God. You may wish to read the story of Moses' birth and early life in Exodus 2. There are many interesting features to explore with the children, such as the fact that his life began in a very unusual way and that he made mistakes along the way before God asked him to do a very special job.

Activity 1: 'Modern-day Moses' and his secret notebook

Many children keep journals or notebooks about things that have happened to them, so the concept of how Moses might record his experiences if he were alive today will be a familiar one. Explain that the notebook in the following story is fictional—not the real thing. The entries are based on the stories found in the book of Exodus, from chapter 3 onwards. The story could be read aloud to the children, or the notebook entries given to different groups of children as a shared reading.

Tuesday

What a day it's been! Just when I was beginning to think everything was settling down! I've finally got myself sorted out with a job. I enjoy being a shepherd. I like roaming the hillsides caring for my father-in-law Jethro's sheep and goats. It gives me lots of time to think. Today I decided the time had come to take the flock across the desert to Sinai, the holy mountain of God.

I knew it would be a long journey so I set off really early. I had no problems along the way and everything went smoothly. I felt happy when I got to the mountain. It's a lovely spot. I settled the animals and then I sat down for a rest.

Suddenly, I saw a flashing light, quite a distance away. I rubbed my eyes—there seemed to be a figure in the middle of a bush that had burst into flames! I was sure the figure was an angel. I looked a second time. The branches were on fire but not being destroyed. I decided to investigate.

I hope nobody reads this notebook because they will never in a million years believe what happened next. When I got a little distance away from the bush, *God* spoke to me! Don't ask me how, but I knew it was him. He said, 'Moses' and I just replied, 'Here I am.' It felt the right thing to say.

God said, 'Don't come any closer. Take off your sandals. The ground you are on is holy ground. I am the God who was worshipped by your ancestors, Abraham, Isaac and Jacob.'

I felt really scared and covered my face with my hands. I could not look at the bush. I was tingling all over.

God told me that he was very upset about the way his people were being treated as slaves in Egypt and how he wanted to rescue them. Then he said he wanted *me* to go to ask the king to release the people.

I cannot write any more tonight. I am just too tired. Have to go to sleep now. My head is throbbing.

Wednesday

It is a fine, warm day today. I feel much more refreshed after a good night's sleep. I have been able to have a good think. I am off to take the sheep to better grazing land now and will write later.

Friday

I did not get a chance to write any more yesterday. A lot more happened.

I told God that I could not go to the king—that I was no leader and I could not bring his people out of slavery.

Then he said, 'I will be with you and you will know that I am the one who sent you.' He told me that I will worship him on this mountain after the people have been led out of Egypt. Next, he told me what to do so that the people would know that I was their new leader and that I would be leading them to freedom. God also told me that he would be making life very difficult for the Egyptians if they refused to release the people.

I was worried that everybody would ignore me and refuse to do as I said. Then something strange happened. I was carrying my walking stick—the one I use to get the sheep out of tricky situations. God said, 'Throw your stick down!' So I did.

I can hardly believe I am writing this, but when it hit the ground it turned into a snake. I was really startled! God told me to pick the snake up by the tail, and, when I did, it turned back into my stick. He told me this would prove to the people that I was to be their leader.

Then he asked me to put my hand into my shirt. When I pulled it out again, it was white and my skin was wrinkled up as if I had leprosy. I was really scared! God told me to put my hand back in my shirt again. The next time I pulled it out, it was back to normal.

God said that if these miracles did not convince the people, I should take some water from the River Nile and pour it on to the ground, where it would turn to blood. I am not sure I like the idea of that!

Anyway, after this I was starting to panic. I begged him to find someone else to do the job. In the end he agreed to let my brother Aaron come with me to help me. I am off to talk to him now.

Thursday

It is a long time since I last wrote in my notebook. It has been so busy and so much has happened to me. I asked Jethro to let me go back to Egypt, and soon Aaron joined me. I told Aaron what God had said and done.

Aaron and I have been to see the king of Egypt. We told him that the slaves must be set free. He would not listen. He then took away all the straw so that when the slaves were making bricks they could not make them properly. There was no straw to be found anywhere and the slaves have been beaten up badly by the Egyptian slave masters. It was a terrible time.

I prayed to God in desperation. I told him that he had done nothing to help us at all. All God said to me after this was that he was God and he would keep his promises. I told the slaves this, but they were feeling so bad by that time that they would not believe me.

I went with Aaron again to tell the king to let the slaves leave Egypt. I told him that God would do all sorts of things to harm his people if he did not let the slaves go. I felt very confused, not really knowing what was going to happen, but somehow I knew that God would keep his word.

A lot happened after this. God sent plagues of frogs, gnats and flies. Then the animals died and skin sores infected the Egyptians and their animals, and then there was a hailstorm. The storm wiped out all the crops, but the king still would not listen.

Next there were swarms of locusts. There have been many arguments with the king and I have learnt to be brave and speak out. I told the king that he could not stop us from worshipping our God. The next time I stretched my hand towards the sky, darkness fell over the whole land. I will have to stop writing now, because I cannot see a thing!

Weeks later

So much has happened, I do not know where to begin. I have not been able to write for so long. Here I am back on Mount Sinai with all God's people—they are my people too. We are free! God has saved us all.

After the darkness fell, God instructed us to tell the people to sacrifice a lamb or young goat and to smear some blood on the two doorposts of each house. He said that, the same night, he would pass through the whole land and that the firstborn of all the Egyptians would be killed, but that we would be safe because he would see the blood on the doorposts. We are to remember this day always. It is to become a special festival for us every year.

At last, after this terrible event, the king finally agreed to let us go. But as I led the people towards the Red Sea, the king changed his mind. He sent his soldiers in their chariots to recapture us. When we got to the seashore, I thought we would all die because the soldiers were getting closer and closer. I cried out to the Lord to save us.

God told me to stretch my arm out over the sea, and suddenly a strong east wind sprang up and split the water. We could see a pathway through the sea. At daybreak the Egyptians tried to follow us, but when I stretched my hand up towards the sky again, the waters rolled back and they were all drowned.

All we can do now is worship the Lord our God. I will go on leading his people.

Activity 2: The Passover

Read the story of the Passover in the Bible (Exodus 12:1–30) and then do one or more of the following activities:

1. Either borrow a county artefacts box or contact the company 'Articles of Faith', who sell many helpful religious artefacts and books for educational use. Visit their website at www.articlesoffaith.co.uk. Prepare the various Passover foods and set out a table with a Seder meal. Re-enact the meal. There is a simple form of the Haggadah or Seder meal on page 42 of *Step into the Story* by Margaret Spivey and Anna Jean (BRF, 2003, priced £15.99).

2. Invite a rabbi from a local synagogue, or another member of the local Jewish community, to come and talk about this important Jewish festival. Find out what it means to them personally in their modern-day lives.

3. Obtain the BBC video *Pathways of Belief—Judaism*, which explores what Jewish families do at the feast of the Passover, and discuss this with the children. (Investigate the BBC website if you do not have a library of video resources in school.) The website address is www.bbc.co.uk.

4. Ask the children if they have been to a special meal or celebration with their friends or families. Was it an important occasion? If so, why? Food and fellowship are important in all the world's religions, in non-faith communities, and in life in general. This is another area for exploration and discussion.

5. Ask a local Roman Catholic or Anglican priest to come into school, or, better still, arrange a visit to your local parish church. Explore how Christians remember the night Jesus celebrated the last supper (which also began as a celebration of the Passover) for himself and his disciples. Find out what the local Christian community call the celebration. It has several names—the Eucharist, Holy Communion, Mass and Lord's Supper.

   Should you wish to extend this into your 'exploring different ways that Christians worship' units, you may wish to invite other Christian leaders into school—for example, a Methodist, United Reformed Church or Baptist minister, or a free church pastor. Ask if the children can interview him or her about their lives, how they came to be working for the church and what changes or impact this has had in their personal lives. It is important that children are encouraged to discover that modern-day people still feel that they want to follow God, lead his people and teach others about him.

Activity 3: Leader profile

Have a discussion, either as a whole class or in small groups, about the qualities Moses possessed. What makes someone a good leader? Are there different types of leaders and different styles of leadership? Is leadership important?

Why did God choose Moses? Moses himself was very doubtful about taking on the role. What gave Moses the strength to persevere? Discuss his strength of faith. Was he ever angry with God?

Follow the discussion by asking the children to complete a leader profile sheet for Moses. To do this, the children need to put Moses' name and job description (such as 'Asked by God to lead the people of Israel out of Egypt') at the top of a sheet of paper. They then think about what he might have looked like and what clothes he would have worn and draw a picture of him in the centre of the paper. Around the figure, ask them to write what qualities he possessed, skills he learned, gifts he discovered he had and qualities of leadership he demonstrated.

Activity 4: Into the unknown

Moses was asked to leave his everyday life and to set off on a dangerous journey back to Egypt. He had to trust God. At first he was not willing to do so. Comparisons can be made with Noah, the stories of saints in Section 2 of this book, and with modern-day leaders. Lead your research into a discussion about why people feel they have to journey into the unknown for a cause that they believe in, religious or otherwise.

Activity 5: Elements of God's power and love

The children could be encouraged to think about how people in the Bible, such as Noah and Moses, became aware of God's power and love. Follow the discussion with ideas about how people have become aware of God's presence throughout history and in the world today, particularly through the elements of fire, water and wind.

Ask the children to write a poem as if they were Moses comparing God's power to the elements, using phrases such as, 'God is as strong and mighty as a burning flame... as majestic as the sun...' and so on. They could decorate their work with illustrations of the elements and put the words to music, using percussion instruments to express the sentiments of the poem.

You may wish to read the children the song Moses and the Israelites sang after they had escaped from Egypt (Exodus 15:1–18).

There are many poems in the Old Testament called Psalms, which the children could explore. Some are prayers asking for help, others are songs of praise. Use the contents page of any Bible to locate the book of Psalms. In the Schools Contemporary English Version, it begins on page 512. This could lead into a discussion about what prayer is (communicating with God), why people in the Bible prayed, and why people pray today.

Jesus on the move!

Bible reference
Luke 2:41–52

Teacher fact file

- In this section we see how Jesus' boyhood and adult life involved pilgrimage and moving to where the work needed to be done.
- When he was twelve years old, he went on a pilgrimage with Mary and Joseph to Jerusalem to celebrate the Passover festival. The story may be found in the Gospel of Luke 2:41–52.
- This event highlights the fact that Jesus was used to mixing with and worshipping with other Jewish friends and neighbours and that this religious journey was obviously very important in their lives.
- Mary and Joseph later found Jesus in the temple. He was talking to the priests and answering their questions. The story tells us that this had a profound effect on them. Mary continued to think about that day long afterwards, and gradually she and Joseph grew more and more sure that there was something very special about Jesus.
- Jerusalem is still a sacred place of pilgrimage for Jews, Christians and Muslims.

Activity 1: Where are you, Jesus?

The following activity is a dramatized reading based on Luke 2:41–52, the story of Jesus in the temple.

CAST

★ Narrator
★ Mary
★ Joseph
★ Jesus
★ Priest

Narrator: It was a very hot day in the city of Jerusalem. Everyone was feeling tired. Mary and Joseph and some of their friends and relatives had just set off on the long journey back to Nazareth. They had been celebrating the feast of the Passover in Jerusalem.

Joseph: What a wonderful time we've had, Mary! It has been a lovely Passover.

Mary: Yes, it has, and it has been great sharing it with our family and friends. It is going to be a long and hot journey home to Nazareth, though. I am feeling weary already. By the way, where is Jesus?

Joseph: Oh, don't worry, he's trailing behind as usual, chatting to his cousins, I expect.

Narrator: Shortly after leaving the city, Mary began to get worried.

Mary: Joseph, I have been asking everyone and no one seems to have seen Jesus. He isn't with his cousins. I am worried that we have lost him.

Joseph: Let's wander back through the group. He'll be trailing along at the back, I'm sure.

Narrator: Mary and Joseph pushed their way back through the large group. Nobody had seen Jesus. They could not find him.

Joseph: Oh, where is that boy? He knows we have to get home. We will have to leave the group and go back into Jerusalem to look for him, Mary.

Mary: I do hope he is all right. Sometimes he makes me *so* cross! I told him to stay with the group.

Narrator: They left the group and walked back into the city. They could not see him anywhere in the streets. They looked everywhere.

Joseph: Where on earth can he be? Wait until I find him. He is in *big* trouble! I don't know where to look next, Mary.

Mary: Let's go and look in the temple. That's about the only place left to look.

Narrator: They made their way back to the temple. When they walked inside, they were both amazed at what they saw.

Joseph: There he is! Look at him, sitting there talking. We have been running around searching for hours and there he sits without a care in the world.

Mary: Sshh! Joseph, be quiet. Listen to him! He has all the priests and teachers round him. Look at how he is listening to them. Oh wait... listen! He's asking them questions.

Narrator: Mary and Joseph stood still and listened for a few minutes.

Mary: I can't believe it. Now they are listening to *him*. My son Jesus is answering their questions.

Narrator: Just then, a priest walked over to Mary and Joseph.

Priest: Excuse me, is that your son over there?

Mary: *(Anxiously)* Yes, it is.

Priest: How old is he?

Joseph: He's twelve, sir. I am so sorry he is bothering you all like this. We were on our way home and we lost him. I will make sure he never bothers you again.

Priest: No, no, it's all right. He amazes us all! How does he know all these things about the holy scriptures? Listen to how he is answering all the questions and talking about it all. He is a very special boy!

Narrator: Shortly after this, Jesus came over to his parents.

Mary: Have you any idea how worried we've been, young man? We have been looking everywhere for you. You should not have left the group like that. You know we have to set off for home. Why have you done this to us?

Narrator: Jesus looked at Mary and Joseph and said:

Jesus: Why did you have to look for me? Didn't you know I would be here in my Father's house?

Narrator: Mary and Joseph felt very confused by his words.

Joseph: I don't know what you mean, young man! Now come on, we have to set off for home, and this time *stay with us*! We'll talk about this more when we get home.

Narrator: Mary and Joseph took Jesus home to Nazareth, where he continued to grow wise and strong and did all that they asked him to do. As he grew older, God was very pleased with him and so was everyone who met him. Mary never forgot that day in the temple in Jerusalem. From that time onwards, she knew that her son was the very special person that God had promised he would be.

Activity 2: Exploring pilgrimages to the Holy Land

Carry out some research with the children to find out more about pilgrimages to Jerusalem and the Holy Land today for Jews and Christians. Jerusalem is also a special place of pilgrimage for Muslims. There are many resource books, videos and CD-ROMs available on the subject of pilgrimage to this part of the world. Contact your local RE Resource Centre for help in finding appropriate resources. You may wish to obtain a copy of the book *The World of Pilgrimage—a guide to the world's most sacred places* by George Target (AA Publications) from your local library.

Pilgrimages to the Holy Land are still important today for many Jews and Christians. If possible, invite someone from your local community who has been on a pilgrimage to the Holy Land. He or she may have photographs or videos to show the children and could talk about what the experience meant to them personally. You may also wish to refer back to the story of Granny Roberts' pilgrimage to the Holy Land on pages 22–24.

Alongside pilgrimages to the Holy Land, you may know of someone who has been on a pilgrimage to Lourdes in France, Walsingham in England, or somewhere of equal significance. You can find out about pilgrimages to Lourdes by visiting the websites of church organizations that arrange trips to the site. The Education Department at the Anglican Shrine in Walsingham (see page 37) can supply resources giving information about the experiences of modern-day pilgrims to the shrine.

Discuss with the children:

- The fact that, as a Jew, pilgrimage was an important part of Jesus' life.
- It would have been a long journey from Nazareth to Jerusalem. Look at a map of Bible lands to see how far they had to travel.
- How might Mary and Joseph have travelled? They probably had to walk most of the way.
- Explore the idea that the journey itself is an important part of any pilgrimage and that commitment and effort are required. The journey is a time of mental and spiritual preparation in anticipation of the experience that will be gained on arrival at the final destination.
- Why were Mary and Joseph surprised when they found Jesus listening and teaching in the temple? Was this an important turning point in Jesus' childhood?
- In what ways might this event have confirmed especially to Mary that the angel Gabriel's words were coming true? (See the story of the annunciation in Luke 1:26–38.) This story is important to Christians because Mary was chosen by God to be the mother of Jesus. In what ways did her decision to say 'yes' to God mark the beginning of a life journey (a pilgrimage) for her and Joseph that was different from the one they had planned?
- Look at paintings or icons of the annunciation together. (You will find a wide selection of paintings on the National Gallery's website, www.nationalgallery.org.uk. Search for 'annunciation' on their site to view the paintings housed at the gallery. *Jesus through Art* by Margaret Cooling (RMEP, 1998) includes an activity based on this story.

Activity 3: Making a prayer journey with beads

You could teach the children about rosary beads and how some Christians use the beads to help them remember events in the life of Jesus and his mother, Mary.

There are numerous books about how to use the rosary. Contact the shrine shop in Walsingham or the Education Department for advice on how to obtain a rosary. Children's rosaries with large coloured beads are also available. Log on to the website www.walsingham.org.uk or call the Education Officer on 01328 824205 for details.

Using Worksheet 14 (p. 93), enlarged to A3 size, children could take each bead in turn and draw in it a picture or symbol of each of the events in Jesus' life. At the bottom they can design their own crucifix.

The beads can represent the following events:

- The annunciation (Luke 1:26–38)
- Mary's visit to Elizabeth (Luke 1:39–56)
- Jesus' birth (Luke 2:1–21)
- Jesus is presented in the temple (Luke 2:22–40)
- Jesus in the temple at the age of twelve (Luke 2:41–52)
- Jesus' baptism (Luke 3:21–22)
- The miracle at the wedding at Cana (John 2:1–12)
- Jesus proclaims the kingdom of God and calls his first disciples (Mark 1:14–20)
- The transfiguration (Mark 9:1–13)
- The last supper (Mark 14:12–26)
- The garden of Gethsemane (Mark 14:32–42)
- Jesus' trial (Mark 14:53–65)
- The crown of thorns (Mark 15:16–19)
- Carrying the cross (Mark 15:20–21)
- The crucifixion (Mark 15:22–41)
- The resurrection (Mark 16:1–8)
- The ascension (Mark 16:19–20)
- Pentecost (Acts 2:1–13)

You will find it helpful to look up the stories in the Bible with the children to trace the life of Jesus in the Gospels. Note that many of the stories appear in all three of the synoptic Gospels (Matthew, Mark and Luke). You may wish to compare the different accounts. The research could stretch over several lessons.

Finally, you may wish to look at some of the parables Jesus told or his miracles of healing to illustrate the fact that Jesus travelled from place to place, teaching and caring for people. Examples include Luke 6:17–19 (preaching and teaching), Mark 8:22–25 (Jesus heals a blind man) and Luke 8:4–15 (the parable of the farmer), but there are many other stories to choose from.

Activity 4: Jesus' last journey

This activity uses the stations of the cross to introduce the story of the first Good Friday when Jesus was brought before the Roman governor, Pilate, then beaten, then made to carry the heavy wood of the cross through the city of Jerusalem.

Background information on the stations of the cross

Christian pilgrims walk the route that Jesus took when he carried his cross through Jerusalem on the way to be crucified. The route is known as the *Via Dolorosa* (the way of pain). Pilgrims walk the route in order to meditate on the suffering of Jesus and to remember how he sacrificed his life for the whole world.

There are pictures on the walls at various points along the route where people can pause, think and pray. The last picture is a reminder that Jesus was raised from the dead on the third day after his crucifixion. The route ends at the Church of the Holy Sepulchre. To follow in the footsteps of Jesus in this way is an important part of a pilgrimage to the Holy Land. The journey is often undertaken during the season of Lent (the 40 days before Easter.)

Many Roman Catholic and Anglican churches display a series of 14 pictures, known as the stations of the cross, around the walls of the church on Good Friday. The pictures depict what happened on the route that Jesus took, and can be used in the following ways:

- Christians walk from picture to picture. They often sing a hymn as they walk.
- They stop at each picture and listen to a portion of scripture that illustrates what is happening to Jesus at that point. They look at the picture and think or pray.
- They often think about particular examples of hardship and pain that people are going through in today's world, or that they are experiencing in their own personal lives, and pray about these issues, situations, or people. This connects the journey of suffering Jesus had to make with journeys of suffering for many in today's world. Christians believe they can tell Jesus all about these things in prayer and he will listen to them and be with them in their suffering.

The stations of the cross traditionally include the following events:

1 Jesus is condemned to die.
2 Jesus carries his cross.
3 Jesus falls for the first time.
4 Jesus meets his mother.
5 Simon helps Jesus carry his cross.
6 Veronica wipes Jesus' face.
7 Jesus falls for the second time.
8 Jesus meets the women of Jerusalem.
9 Jesus falls for the third time.
10 Jesus is stripped of his garments.
11 Jesus is nailed to the cross.
12 Jesus dies on the cross.
13 Jesus is taken down from the cross.
14 Jesus is laid in the tomb.

There is often an additional picture showing Jesus being raised from the dead. There are many examples of the stations of the cross available to view on the Internet, or in books from Christian bookshops or RE Resource Centres. Carry out research into the stations of the cross and discuss the images together, comparing traditional and contemporary styles. When you have completed the research, the children could then use Worksheet 15 (p. 94) to design their own images of the stations of the cross on a sheet of paper marked into 14 (or 15) sections.

Activity 5: An Easter drama

The children could create a tableau, piece of drama, dance or mime with their own written narrative to present the stations of the cross to others in the school. This is particularly poignant in the lead-up to Easter and will supplement the QCA RE unit about Easter. If appropriate in any individual school, children may also wish to compile prayers to accompany each station.

There is an inspiring CD called *Born for This* which contains a dramatized musical presentation of the stations of the cross for schools (produced by CJM Music). You can order it from their website, www.cjmmusic.fsnet.co.uk/catalogue. Children can make up their own drama to go with the tracks. CJM also perform this and a variety of other creative musical workshops in schools. See their website for more information.

Part 4

Jesus chooses his first disciples

Bible reference
Luke 5:1–11

Teacher fact file

- This unit explores how Peter came to be a follower of Jesus and shows how the first friends of Jesus (his disciples) found the course of their lives changed when they chose to follow him.
- Their decision to go with Jesus meant being prepared to make journeys and undertake challenging deeds.
- Peter and his friends must leave their homes and families to begin a journey into the unknown. They have no clues to where they will end up but they know that they must do it.
- This is another powerful example of how ordinary people (like Noah and Moses in the Old Testament) are chosen by God.

Focus

Read the following story aloud to the children to set the scene.

My name is Simon Peter and I am a fisherman. It's hard work, but I enjoy my job. I like the fresh air and I have some great friends to work alongside. I've been fishing since I was a boy and I never thought I would ever do anything else. This week, though, something happened that was to change my life for ever. Let me tell you all about it.

Last Monday began like any other day. I was sitting on the shore of Lake Gennesaret with my partners, James and John. We were washing our nets. Jesus, the preacher from Nazareth, was a little way along the shore from us. He had been talking to crowds of people for some time. We were enjoying listening to him as we worked. My boat was one of two boats moored up on the shore of the lake.

Suddenly, Jesus walked towards my boat and climbed into it. I jumped up quickly, wondering what he wanted. He said to me, 'Row your boat a little way out into the water, please, Simon!' I was a little surprised by this request, but I decided to do as he said. I rowed the boat out until we were a little way from the shore.

By this time, all the people had walked to the water's edge and were crowding round. Jesus sat down in the boat and carried on telling the people about God. I felt a little impatient, because I had so much work to get on with, and here I was stuck out in the water! But as Jesus told his stories, I started to really enjoy listening to him. Then he turned to me and said, 'Simon, row the boat out into deep water and let your nets down to catch some fish.' I was rather taken aback—it seemed a silly thing to do.

'Master,' I said to him, 'we've been working all night and we have not caught a single fish!' Then I added, 'But if that's what you want me to do, then I will do it.'

I cast the nets into the water. After a minute or so, I could not believe my eyes. The nets were so full of fish that they were beginning to tear apart. I called for James and John to come

and help me. They brought their boat alongside mine and together we pulled the nets up. I have never seen so many fish in one catch. We filled both boats.

'We're sinking!' yelled John. The boats were weighed down by so many fish.

Suddenly, I had a strange feeling in my stomach: I just knew that Jesus was special. I felt so small and ashamed. I knelt down in front of him and said, 'Lord, don't come near me. I am a sinful man.' I thought about all the things I'd done wrong in the past. When I saw all those fish, I knew that he had been sent by God and I could trust him completely. We were all so surprised about what had happened. The people standing on the shore just stood in silence.

Jesus spoke to me. He said, 'Simon, don't be afraid. From now on you will bring in people instead of fish.' We pulled the boats up on the shore. Jesus' words sounded very strange, but I knew what he meant. He wanted James, John and me to follow him and help him in his work, bringing people to God. This can mean only one thing—we must leave our jobs and our families and go with him on his travels. We do not know for how long or what will happen in the future, but we know that this is what we must do.

Why me, though? Some of my friends think we are crazy. I never thought I would ever do something like this. What extraordinary times!

Discussion starters

What do the children think about the choice that Peter and his friends made? Can you think of anyone who has acted in a similar way in recent times? In what ways might people be prepared to give up the familiarity of their everyday lives to serve Jesus?

Activity 1: Act it out!

The children could create a piece of dance or drama to tell the story of the call of the first disciples.

Activity 2: Internet quest

Carry out Internet research to find out about missionary organizations and aid agencies such as Church Mission Society, USPG, Christian Aid and the Red Cross—there are many more to discover. Many organizations can supply information packs, videos and resources to help with project work.

Visit the *UK Christian Handbook* website for information about organizations and agencies at www.ukchristianhandbook.org.uk.

Encourage the children to find out about people who have left their jobs and everyday lives to go to other countries to help run projects for people without enough food, water or medical care.

The children could also find out about people who follow Jesus in other ways, such as those who are called to a vocation as a monk, nun or priest. Find out about religious orders in your locality. You may be able to arrange for a monk or a nun to come into school to talk to the children.

When you have completed your research, make a wall display about ways in which people follow Jesus today.

The story of Paul

Bible reference
Acts 9:1–19

Teacher fact file

- Paul was a Jew and was known as Saul before he became a follower of Jesus. We learn about him in the book of Acts, and through the letters he wrote to the early churches.
- We first meet him in Acts 7:58 as a young official present at the death of a Christian called Stephen, who was stoned to death for his faith.
- We are told that Saul 'approved' the stoning of Stephen (Acts 8:1–2) and that, after Stephen's death, he went around church communities in Jerusalem arresting Christians.
- He became a Christian himself after a dramatic encounter with the risen Jesus while he was travelling on the road from Jerusalem to Damascus.
- After his conversion, he dedicated his life to his Christian faith and travelled to many places, spreading the gospel of Jesus.

Activity 1: Blinded by the light!

The following activity is a dramatized story about the day Paul became a Christian. It illustrates how the Christian story journeyed onwards after Jesus' death, resurrection and ascension into heaven.

CAST

- ★ Narrator
- ★ Saul (later known as Paul)
- ★ Jesus
- ★ Friend 1
- ★ Friend 2
- ★ Ananias

Narrator: Saul was born into a Jewish family. He believed in God but he did not believe that Jesus was God's son. He was not happy about all the followers of Jesus—this new faith seemed such a threat to his own religious beliefs. He started to make a lot of trouble for the new church, arresting as many Christians as possible and putting them in prison. Some were even killed.

One day, Saul set off on a journey to a place called Damascus. He planned to travel with two of his friends.

Saul: Not far to go now. I can see Damascus in the distance. Let's walk faster. I want to get there as quickly as possible to deliver these letters to the Jewish leaders.

Friend 1: What are the letters about, Saul?

Saul: They are about all the groups of Christians who are meeting together everywhere. We must stop them!

Friend 2: That man Jesus seems to have many followers, even though he's dead. They say he rose from the dead, you know, and that he has now gone back to heaven.

Saul: Yes, they seem to be spreading some dangerous tales. I intend to put a stop to such nonsense.

Narrator: Suddenly a bright light shone down from heaven, right into Saul's eyes. It was so dazzling that he fell down on his knees and covered his eyes with both hands. Then he heard a voice saying:

Jesus: Saul! Saul! Why are you so cruel to me?

Narrator: Saul felt very frightened. He called out:

Saul: Who are you?

Narrator: Thc voice answered:

Jesus: I am Jesus. I am the one you are so cruel to. Now get up and go into the city, where you will be told what to do.

Narrator: Saul's two friends were shocked. They had heard the voice too, but they had not seen anyone. They did not know what to say. They helped Saul to his feet. He still had his eyes tightly shut, and when he opened them he was very scared.

Saul: I can't see! I can't see! Help me, please! What has happened to me? I am blind!

Narrator: His friends took hold of his hands and led him into Damascus. For three days he could not eat or drink, and he still could not see anything at all. In Damascus, a follower of Jesus called Ananias had a strange dream in which he heard Jesus speaking to him.

Jesus: Ananias, can you hear me?

Ananias: Lord, here I am.

Jesus: Get up and go to the house of Judas in Straight Street. You will find a man called Saul from Tarsus there. He is praying. He has had a strange dream too. He has dreamt about you, Ananias. In his dream he saw you put your hands on him and then he could see again.

Narrator: Ananias had heard about Saul and felt troubled.

Ananias: Lord, I have heard about lots of terrible things that Saul has done to your followers in Jerusalem. Now the chief priests have given him permission to come here to arrest anyone who is a follower of yours.

Narrator: Jesus answered:

Jesus: Ananias, go now! I have chosen Saul to tell kings, and all people in Israel, about me. I will show him how much he must go through for being a follower of mine.

Narrator: Ananias did what Jesus had asked him to do. He went to the house and found Saul there. He put his hands on him and said:

Ananias: Saul, the Lord Jesus has sent me. He appeared to you on the road and he wants you to be able to see again and to be filled with the Holy Spirit.

Narrator: Straight away something amazing happened to Saul.

Saul: I can see! I can see!

Narrator: Saul rubbed his eyes and suddenly he could see again. As soon as he got up, he was baptized and became a follower of Jesus. He then ate some food and began to feel much better.

Saul: I must tell everyone about Jesus. He is the Son of God. I must travel to as many places as I can, so that more people will become his followers.

Narrator: After this, Saul (who became known as Paul) travelled far and wide, teaching many people about Jesus. He had many adventures and at times found himself in some very frightening and dangerous situations. Hundreds of years later, the church made him a saint because he had obeyed God and committed his life to serving him and to sharing the good news about Jesus.

Activity 2: Painting St Paul

This activity is designed to help children find out about the way that Paul has been depicted in art through the ages.

Make a collection of postcards showing examples of paintings, icons or statues of St Paul. For information, contact the shrine shop in Walsingham, Norfolk by visiting www.walsinghamanglican.org.uk, the Anglican shrine's website. You might like to collect sets of postcards, or reasonably priced wooden mounted icon prints of Jesus, or various saints or biblical events, for your resources collection in school, or to make a display of ways in which Christianity has been passed on from one generation to the next through art.

Activity 3: Discussion starters

The children can be encouraged to talk about how Saul's life was suddenly changed by his experience on the road to Damascus. Why do they think Jesus chose Saul to help him spread the gospel message? Can you think of modern-day examples of a similar conversion? Comparisons may also be made to the other stories about people who had extraordinary religious experiences in Section 2 of this book, or modern-day examples about people whose lives have been changed. The book *The Cross and the Switchblade* by David Wilkerson (Zondervan, 2002) is a good example of lives being completely changed through the Christian faith.

You may wish to contact the Church Army at www.churcharmy.org.uk and ask them to suggest officers who might be available to come in to school to speak about their work in prisons or with the homeless. Alternatively, there may be Church Army officers who have experienced life-changing events due to their own personal faith, who would be available to give you more information, or to visit the school. Similarly, you may wish to contact your local Salvation Army Citadel through their main website, www.salvationarmy.org, to arrange a visit from a member of their organization. There may even be hostels or day centres for the homeless in your locality which would be able to arrange a visit for the children to meet members of staff who have become involved in the work because of their conversion to the Christian faith. This needs to be carefully researched and planned with the organization concerned.

Alternatively, there may be local Christians who

have responded to God in perhaps less dramatic ways, who would be prepared to come in to school to talk about what their faith means to them. Decide with your speaker in advance how you would like to construct the interview or talk. Ask the children to prepare questions in advance.

Paul's conversion was to lead to a complete change of lifestyle, and he went on to travel widely and endure hardship in order to teach others about Jesus. What do the children feel about this? Can people's lives really be changed by God? The children could use Worksheet 16 (p. 95) to write their thoughts around the picture. When they have completed the exercise, they could colour in the picture. The finished work could then form part of a class display.

Activity 4: Look it up!

Paul's adventures are recorded in the book of Acts. Paul travelled widely, teaching people about Jesus and helping them to form churches and grow in their faith. Older children may enjoy researching information about the events of Paul's life for themselves. When they have read the story, they could then write it in their own words, taking the part of one of the characters, writing the story as a poem, or turning it into a simple play or storyboard. Suggested events include:

1. Where did Saul (Paul) and Barnabas travel to first? (Acts 13:1–52)
2. What happened in Lystra? (Acts 14:8–20)
3. Paul goes to prison. (Acts 16:16–40)
4. What is love? (1 Corinthians 13:1–13)
5. Paul talks about what he believes. (Philippians 1:12–26)

Activity 5: Reporting about Paul

Ask the children to imagine they are journalists for a magazine. They have to interview Paul and write an article about his conversion and some of his adventures and his work. This also opens up the opportunity for children to discuss with one another how this sort of experience would affect a person. How would Paul feel about it? What would be the reaction of those around him?

If desired, explore further the fact that sudden conversions to Christianity still happen in people's lives today. Give examples if possible.

Worksheets

'Journey of life' wheel

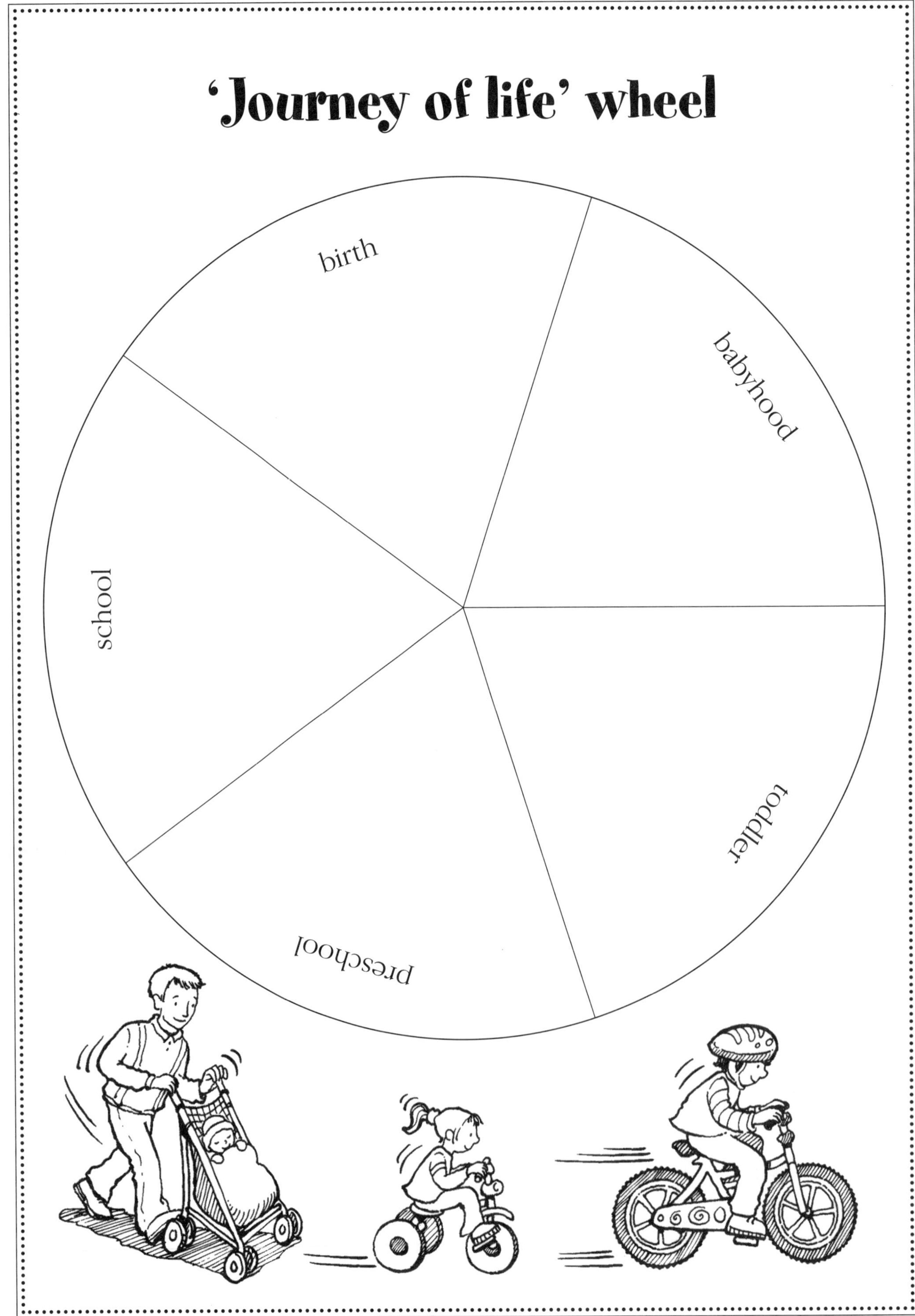

I'm a star!

Master Cedric: a picture for you to colour

Do we need safe places (sanctuaries)?

The Sanctuary Knocker on the north door of Durham Cathedral is a symbol of holiness and safety (sanctuary). No one can tear the ring from the powerful lion's mouth! What words would you use to describe this symbolism?

The cross reminds Christians that Jesus died on the cross to bring people back into a relationship with God and that he rose from death and is now in heaven, hearing their prayers. What words would you use to describe this symbolism?

What other special symbols are you familiar with? Draw them here.

Design your own special symbol to represent something important to you in the space below.

The Walsingham legend

Create your own storyboard as the legend unfolds.

Come to the water!

Oh come to the water, for we will tell
Of the wonders of St Winifred's well,
A tale that runs like the crystal stream
Around the pool so deep and clean.
Oh come to the water, those who seek
To know about a girl so sweet
Who did not want to marry the tribal chief
So ran away to find her peace.

Oh come to the water, don't delay,
We'll tell what happened on that day
When Caradoc chased after her
To tell her just how much he cared.
But when he got there, she said, 'No,
I cannot be your wife, now go.'

Oh come to the water, hear how he
So wanted her his wife to be,
He drew his sword, struck off her head.
Poor Winifred, she now was dead.

Oh come to the water that rose up high
Where Winifred did fall and die.
The ground it opened far and wide
And swallowed Caradoc inside!

Oh come to the water where Beuno stood,
Alarmed to see this sea of blood.
He grabbed her head, then rubbed his eyes,
For Winifred to life did rise!

Oh come to the water, pure and clear ,
As pilgrims have for many a year.
Remember those who suffer pain
And pray they may be well again.

Goosey! Goosey!

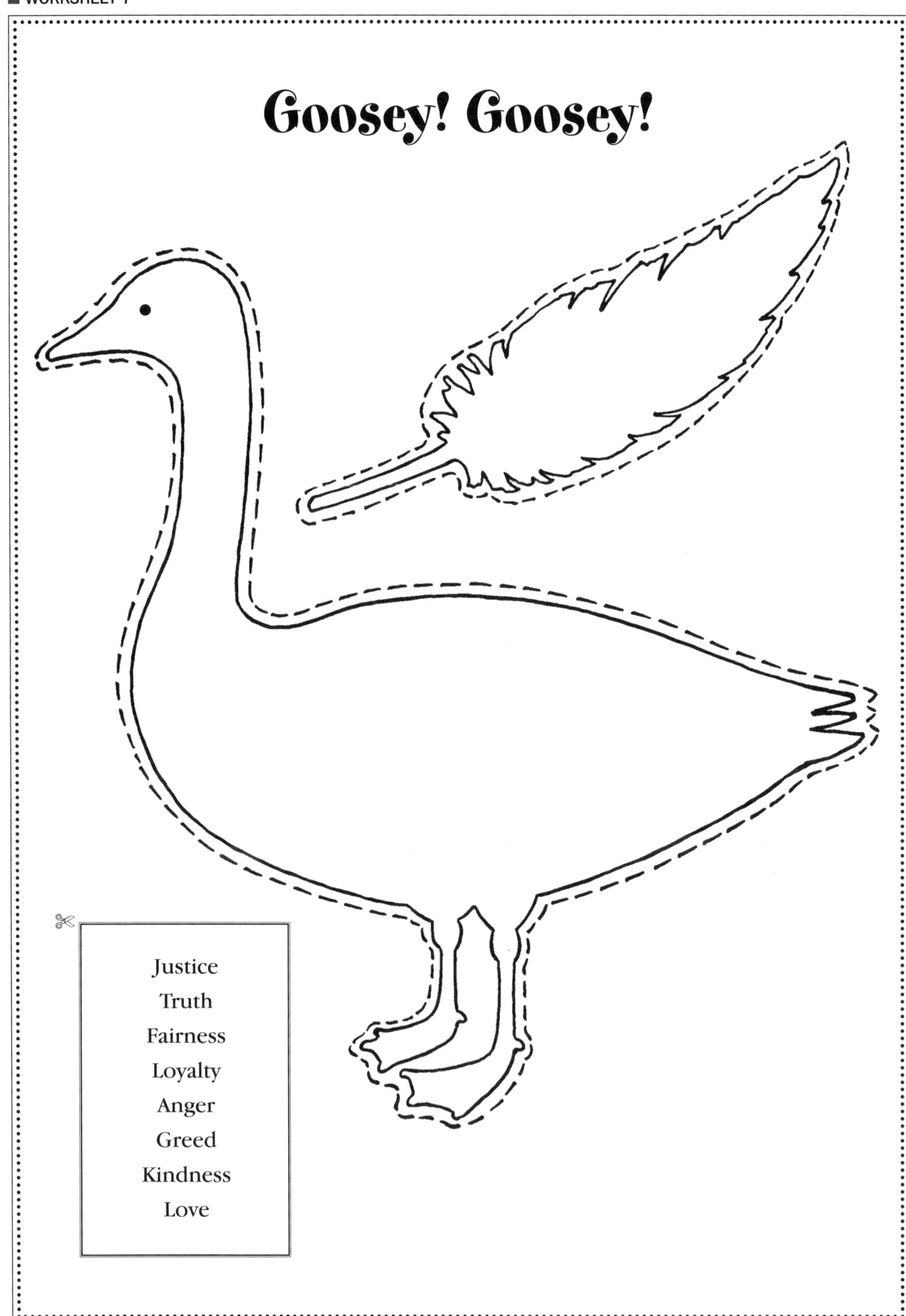

St Hugh fact file

St Hugh: What would you do?

1. Your best mate is being bullied by someone you are friendly with in your class. This person invites you to their party. Then, at playtime, in front of you they push your best friend around. What should you do?
   a) Stand up to them and go and report them to your teacher?
   b) Walk away and pretend you did not see it happen?
   c) Don't report them, but decide not to go to the party?

2. You find out that your friend is ill-treating their pet cat. The cat seems to be in a terrible state. Would you...
   a) Talk to your friend about it and threaten to report them the RSPCA?
   b) Ignore it: you don't want to fall out with your friend?
   c) Ring the RSPCA anonymously without telling your friend?

3. A boy from a family of asylum seekers joins your class. He cannot speak any English and lots of children are making fun of him. You feel upset about this but your mates say you are stupid to want to be his friend. Do you...
   a) Wait until after school, then offer to walk home with the boy and be kind to him when your friends are out of the way?
   b) Ignore your mates and just start getting to know him and be his friend?
   c) Ignore him and go along with the others?

4. Your grandma is being forced out of her house where she has lived for 40 years. The local council want to demolish it. She is very upset and does not want to go into an old people's home. Your mum says there is nothing you can do. Do you...
   a) Just leave it as it is—there is nothing you can do?
   b) Find out about how to write to your MP, or go and see him or her, to see if they can help?
   c) Tell your grandma you will help her write to the council, your MP and a solicitor, and go to the Citizens Advice Bureau for advice?

5. You are out in town with your friends. Suddenly one of them suggests that you all spray graffiti on the wall behind a local supermarket. No one will see you and it sounds like fun. You do not feel this is right, but do you...
   a) Just go along with it because you do not want to look a fool and lose your mates?
   b) Tell them, 'No, this is wrong' and walk away from them straight away?
   c) Try to reason with them and say that it's a stupid thing to do and if they continue you will have to report it to the shop owner and tell your parents when you get home.

A Celtic Christian prayer

Decorate the first letter of the prayer in the box provided and then add your own lines to the prayer in the space provided, with each line beginning with the words, 'Deep peace…'

Deep peace of the running wave
Deep peace of the flowing air
Deep peace of the shining stars
Deep peace of the quiet earth
Deep peace of the Prince of Peace
To you and yours.

TRADITIONAL, AUTHOR UNKNOWN

Deep peace… ____________________

Deep peace… ____________________

Deep peace… ____________________

Deep peace… ____________________

Deep peace… ____________________

Design a Celtic cross

Look at the patterns on the smaller cross in the picture and then create your own pattern in the cross template provided.

He has no name

Using the verses as your inspiration, design and draw symbols that illustrate the theme of this poem, and then create a border to decorate the poem.

Voices, footsteps heard each day
Some don't look, they just pass by.
Clicking cameras, finding tombs,
Glancing at watches, hurrying on.

A ring of poppies marks the spot,
Their petals red like the blood he shed.
He has no name, but he was brave
And died that day in France.

Some voices stop and feet stand still
Upon the polished marble spot.
They think of wars in days gone by
And fighting that goes on today.

He has no name so we don't know
Who he was, rich or poor,
Or what he'd say about that day,
He died for king and country.

Rainbow messages

Making a prayer journey with beads

With a partner or in a group, read the stories about the different stages of Jesus' life from the New Testament part of the Bible. Then design a symbol or draw a picture in each bead shape to represent what happened to Jesus at each stage.

Jesus' last journey

Design your own images of the stations of the cross.

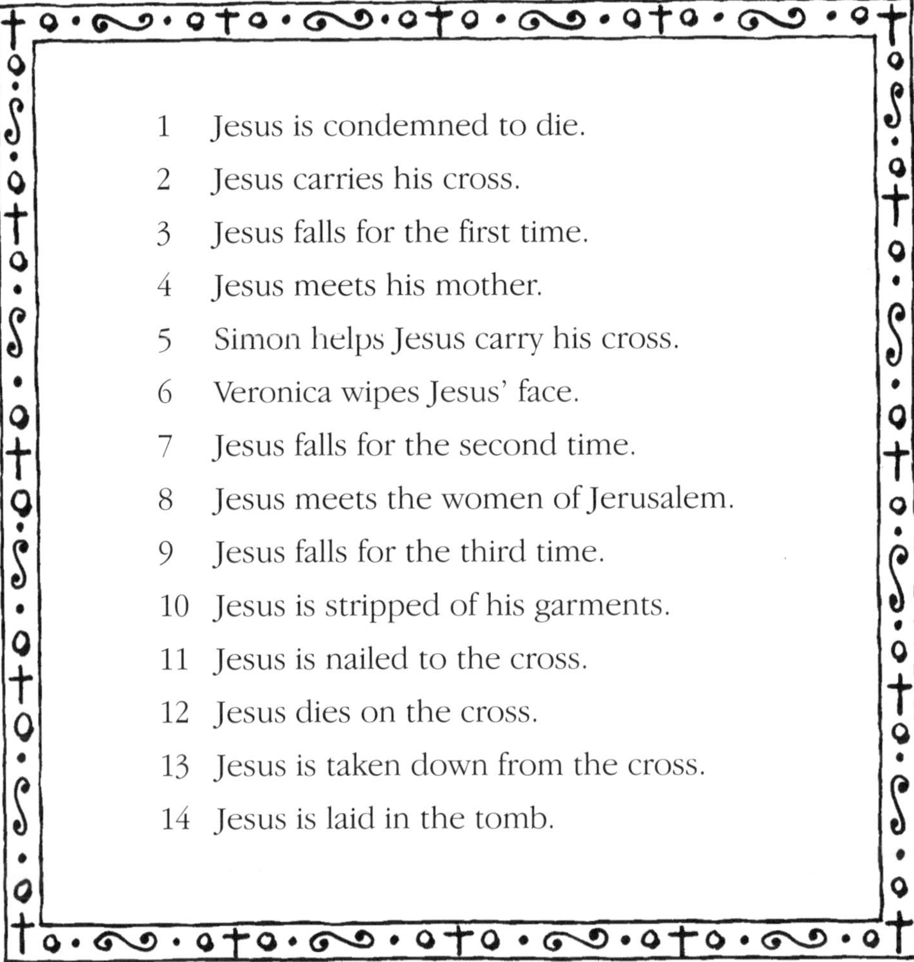

1 Jesus is condemned to die.
2 Jesus carries his cross.
3 Jesus falls for the first time.
4 Jesus meets his mother.
5 Simon helps Jesus carry his cross.
6 Veronica wipes Jesus' face.
7 Jesus falls for the second time.
8 Jesus meets the women of Jerusalem.
9 Jesus falls for the third time.
10 Jesus is stripped of his garments.
11 Jesus is nailed to the cross.
12 Jesus dies on the cross.
13 Jesus is taken down from the cross.
14 Jesus is laid in the tomb.

Spotlight on Paul

Can people's lives really be changed by God? Write words around the picture to describe your thoughts about Paul's conversion to Christianity, or the experience of other people you have learned about or met. What words could you use to describe their experiences, or to describe your own thoughts about this? When you have completed your work, colour in the picture.

Bibliography

Many of the following publications may be useful for further information and photographs.

Contemporary English Version: Schools Bible (Harper Collins/The Bible Societies, ISBN 0 00 7103000 X)

Sacred Places, Pilgrim Paths: an Anthology of Pilgrimage, Martin Robinson (Zondervan, 1988)

To Be a Pilgrim: a Spiritual Notebook, Basil Hume OSB (Triangle, 1988)

The World of Pilgrimage: a Guide to the World's Most Sacred Places, George Target (AA,1997)

Oxford Dictionary of Saints (Oxford University Press, 2004)

Sacred Britain, Martin Palmer and Nigel Palmer (Piatkus, 1997)

Pilgrim Ways: Catholic Pilgrimage Sites in Britain and Ireland, David Alton (St Paul's Publishing, 2002)

Pod and Ezzie on Pilgrimage, Janet Marshall (Kevin Mayhew, 2003)

Pilgrims and Pilgrimages, Janet Marshall (Education Dept, Shrine OLW, Knight St, Walsingham, NR22 6EF)